A Cup of Comfort

for Christians

Inspirational Stories of Faith

EDITED BY
MARGARET AND JAMES BELL

ADAMS MEDIA

Avon, Massachusetts

Published by
Adams Media, an F+W Publications Company
57 Littlefield Street, Avon, MA 02322. U.S.A.
www.adamsmedia.com and *www.cupofcomfort.com*
ISBN 13: 978-1-59337-541-6
ISBN 10: 1-59337-541-7

Printed in Canada.

J I H G F E D C B

Library of Congress Cataloging-in-Publication Data
is available from the publisher.

This publication is designed to provide accurate and authoritative information
with regard to the subject matter covered. It is sold with the understanding that
the publisher is not engaged in rendering legal, accounting, or other professional
advice. If legal advice or other expert assistance is required, the services of a
competent professional person should be sought.
　　—From a *Declaration of Principles* jointly adopted by a Committee of the
American Bar Association and a Committee of Publishers and Associations

Many of the designations used by manufacturers and sellers to distinguish
their products are claimed as trademarks. Where those designations appear in
this book and Adams Media was aware of a trademark claim, the designations
have been printed with initial capital letters.

This book is available at quantity discounts for bulk purchases.
For information, please call 1-800-289-0963

I dedicate this book to my long-time friend Sally Oxley,
who has blessed my life more than she can know;
and to Sharon Ritchie and Mary Alice Burdett,
my new sisters (in-law) whom I love.

Nor do I wish to forget
my Thursday morning ladies prayer group,
who keep me walking close to God.
– MB

To my father, James Stuart Bell, Senior –
a dedicated servant of the Lord,
a lifelong model of wisdom and love.

To my mother, Kathryn T. Bell,
a woman of class and character who has been
an encouragement and "cup of comfort"
to me along the journey.
—JB

Acknowledgments

To Michal Needham, who did a superb job in helping with the administration, arrangement, and editing of the manuscript. Thanks once again to the ever capable editorial direction of Kate Epstein, who has a heart as well as a head for these inspirational stories. Gary Krebs, the publisher, has continued to be an advocate for a significant Christian presence in this series, and for that Margaret and I are most grateful.

 Contents

Introduction

An old eighteenth-century hymn states, "God works in mysterious ways, his wonders to perform." The unusual ways that God works in our lives are certainly beyond our comprehension. In fact, in the Book of Isaiah, it says that, "As the heavens are higher than the earth, so are my ways higher than your ways and my thoughts higher than your thoughts." This is a book that is filled with stories of the great variety of ways that ordinary individuals experience God's extraordinary blessings.

Although God richly blesses us in every way (physically, materially, and spiritually), as long as we live in this world, we will experience all kinds of trouble and hardship. It is perhaps during those times of waiting on God with no answers that his ways seem most mysterious. Yet in the end he comes through for those who have a faith that doesn't waver, and he brings good out of the bad. "We know that God works all things for the good of those who love him, who have been called according to his purpose" (Romans 8:28).

For me, reading each story in this volume felt like entering into the most intimate part of each person's life, sharing his or her most sacred moments. These were the moments when Jesus was most tangible and real—when he says, "Where two or three are gathered in my name, there I am in the midst of them." His presence in this book was like a cup of cold water in the midst of many desert experiences.

One of my favorite stories, the opening story in this book, demonstrates the vast scope of God's plan in our lives and why hope and trust in his ultimate purposes is so important. A serviceman who was a foster child marries a girl from Thailand with the hope of starting a true family of his own. After receiving a new assignment in the United States, he returns home alone, his wife to follow soon. Tragically, she dies in childbirth before she leaves Thailand. Twenty-five years later, he returns to her gravesite and there encounters his daughter, the child he assumed had perished with her mother. The daughter revealed that her mother had a medical condition that made having children life threatening. She had not told her husband because she so wanted to fulfill his dreams of having a family. As daughter and father tearfully embraced, he realized his wife had performed the ultimate sacrifice to fulfill his dreams, and he now had a daughter to enjoy after all those years. God does indeed work in mysterious ways.

In these stories, God works in supernatural ways and also in quiet, ordinary ways. He unfolds, as the Bible says, beauty out of ashes; he brings healing, comfort, hope, and joy out of seemingly impossible situations. When God works in the lives of his people, those lives are forever changed. Hearts are mended. Relationships are restored. Bodies are healed. Faith is strengthened. After reading these stories, I felt that God has blessed my heart with greater faith and love, a greater sense of his compassionate responses, and a more sympathetic understanding of our human frailty.

Just as God eventually answered the deepest needs and longings of those within these pages, I wish you, the reader, to experience the blessing of Psalm 20, verse 4: "May He grant your heart's desire and fulfill all your plans."

—*Margaret Bell*

The Ultimate Sacrifice

People who didn't grow up the way I did, in a foster home, can't understand what it's like not to have a family. Without a place to call home, I always felt that I was somehow *less* than other people.

My counselor in high school was the first to show me how to come to terms with my feelings of inferiority. He told me to accept my situation and my life the way it was: accept that I will never have that "family of origin," as he called it, and move on. Then I was to create the concept of my "family of destiny," and make that idea a part of my life now: hold it, care for it, nurture it, and keep it in my heart until I was old enough to accomplish it. Although it wouldn't be a family of origin, I could have a family, a real family all the same. He told me to have faith that it would happen, but also to understand that whatever God gives me is all that I need. God had already given me foster parents who were Christians, and faith was their gift to me. But it would take many, many years for me to realize that faith truly is all I need.

I was eighteen years old, with high school graduation a month away. My foster parents and I knew that I might be drafted and sent to the front lines of the war in Vietnam. As Christians, we opposed the war, so we started looking for alternatives. We learned that if I joined the Air Force, not only would I fulfill my military obligation and not have to worry about the draft, but I would also be safe from direct involvement in the war.

My four-year enlistment in the Air Force began in November 1971. The first three years were spent stateside, but just before my fourth year, I got orders sending me to Thailand. While stationed there, I fell in love with a young Thai woman named Surapun.

Su and I shared our Christian faith—not a common one in Thailand at that time. She was the happiest woman I had ever met. We held hands and even kissed in public, though that was strictly taboo according to Thai custom. But as the love of my life, Su cared more about our relationship and our being content than she did about cultural rules and regulations. I told her of my feelings about being a foster child and my dream of a family of destiny. The idea of helping to fulfill my dreams by starting a family together seemed to only add to Su's happiness.

Surapun and I were so in love, we decided to get married and start our family right away. As a military bride, she would have to undergo a complete physical examination to see if she needed any medical attention. A few days after our small military wedding, Surapun underwent a morning-long battery of tests and X-rays to make sure she was healthy. My wife came home with her typical broad smile, assuring me she was fine and we could start our family immediately.

Three months later, I received orders to return to the United States. But Surapun didn't come with me right away. It would be a long time before she would be able to visit her friends and family once we left Thailand, so I returned to the United States alone. Su would say her proper good-byes and join me soon.

About a month after I arrived at my stateside assignment in Nevada, I got a letter from Surapun telling me she had visited a doctor the day before, but not to worry, everything was fine. In fact, everything was great—she was pregnant! I was happy beyond words.

Over the next few weeks I sent several letters to Su along with some paperwork for her immigration, but a long time went by with no response. Keeping in mind this was her first pregnancy and she might not be feeling well enough to get back to me, I remained patient.

But so much time passed with no word from Surapun that I began to wonder if she'd changed her mind about leaving Thailand. The thought of that was bad enough, but anything worse was unthinkable. Within a few weeks, though, I got a letter from Surapun's mother telling me that my wife had died. Her funeral had already been held two weeks earlier.

My dream of a family of destiny was shattered. The love of my life had perished, and our baby, our creation of love, had perished with her. Although my faith didn't die with Surapun, I found little comfort in it. I continued to go through the motions, but inside I kept asking God, *"Why?"* I prayed for Him to take me too, because I no longer wanted to live.

All this happened in 1975, just before my discharge from the Air Force. I was very young then, and having a spouse die wasn't something I ever thought I'd experience. In the years after Su's death, something kept gnawing at me. I felt the same way I would imagine the parents of a missing child feel. They keep saying that they know she's safe somewhere. They always hold out hope that she's alive, but deep down, they feel the truth. They know she's really dead, but they can experience true closure only when they see her body. It was the same for me. For years I held onto that little glimmer of hope that Su was alive. Deep down, I knew Su was dead, but I wouldn't be able to truly close that chapter of my life until I went back to Thailand and saw her grave for myself. Part of me wanted closure, but part of me really wanted that sliver of hope to live forever. I was torn. The U.S. government discouraged Americans from going anywhere in Southeast Asia for a long time after the Vietnam War was over, so that gave me the out I thought I wanted.

The possibility that Surapun wasn't dead, lingered with me for twenty-five years until I just had to know for sure. In 2000, I finally returned to Thailand to visit her grave. As the nonstop flight from Atlanta touched down on the runway in Bangkok, I gazed out the plastic window at the dense cedar forest that ran alongside the airstrip. I got off the plane quickly and walked the red-carpeted corridor into the crowded terminal.

On to the busy city street in front of the airport, I looked around wistfully. Bangkok looked the same as it had before. It smelled the same, it sounded the same—but it just wasn't the same as when I was here with Su so many years ago.

I flagged down a taxi to take me to the Kump-awappee Field, where Surapun's grave was. By the time we got to the suburbs of Bangkok near Sura-pun's burial site, I began to feel anxious as the hot summer breeze whipped briskly through the windows of the taxi. How would it feel to finally see her grave for myself?

I also thought about why God had punished me all my life, even though I had kept my faith. That's the way it seemed, anyway. I had been raised by a decent family but had still felt inferior because they were not *my* family. When I had attempted to make a family of my own, that was taken away too. I couldn't understand why.

I was still thinking about that when the taxi entered Kumpawappee Field. My senses were nearly overcome by the aromatic flowers and pungent spices that Thais use to decorate graves. My throat burned slightly as I exited the taxi.

I found Surapun's grave. As I stood there, shivers went up my spine, and I had goose bumps on my arms. My hands started shaking and my eyes filled with tears. I stood there looking at her tomb, replaying in my mind some of the times we'd spent together a quarter of a century ago. Her happy smile and her laughter, the way we had let everyone see our love for each other in spite of cultural constraints—it all came back to me.

I bowed my head in prayer, and a tear trickled off my cheek and onto the white marble slab at my feet. While I was praying, I felt a soothing warmth slowly come over me. I felt comfort like I hadn't felt in a long time. Suddenly, I had peace. Su was there, and I was here; we were apart and yet together. For twenty-five years I had longed to feel this close to her. My prayers continued to flow out of my heart as I rejoiced that God had uplifted part of me into the domain where Surapun now was with Him.

Then a young woman walked up beside me and reverently put her hands up, her thumbs touching her nose and her fingertips on her forehead. In the Thai custom, she curtsied as if paying homage to the occupant of the grave.

"Did you know her?" I asked curiously.

"No, I never knew her," she said, "but when I feel lonely, I come here and talk to her."

"Then you must have known her," I answered.

"No, but I will spend the rest of my life wishing I could have known her. She was a wonderful woman. Without her courage and sacrifice, I would not be here."

"What do you mean?"

"When she married, the doctor told her she should not have children because of a medical condition she had, but she told her husband everything was fine. Having a baby could kill her if everything didn't go exactly right, and she lived so far from the base hospital. And everything did not go exactly right."

My head was spinning as reality set in. *No! She must be talking about someone else. She has the wrong grave. Please, God, don't let her say what she's about to say.*

Then she said it. "This woman sacrificed herself so everyone else would be happy. Her mother wanted grandchildren, her husband wanted children. She had concern only for others, never for herself. I love her so much. I'm the cause of her death, and that makes me so sad."

The woman covered her face with her hands and began crying hysterically. "Oh, I love her so much," she wailed.

I closed my eyes and shook my head. This was the daughter my wife had given me, to make my life complete so I would never feel inferior again. But it had taken years for the dream to come to fruition, and it was Su's own mother, probably in a tearful quandary, who had delayed it. She let me assume that both Surapun and the baby had died because she feared I would come and take her grandchild away, the child that I was now holding tightly in my arms. Suddenly I realized that God had not been punishing me. Even though it had taken twenty-five years, God had brought me here to fulfill my dream of a family. My faith had not been in vain; it was instantly renewed.

As my daughter and I stood clutching each other in that graveyard, together at last, I was amazed at what my wife had done. She had set aside her own needs and made the ultimate sacrifice for the well-being of everybody else, but then, Christians live in the shadow of Someone who committed that same act, so many centuries ago.

—*Larkin Huey*

A Closed Door and an Open Window

Our little house was really shaping up. At less than 700 square feet, it had a homey feel that made it just right for our family. We'd sold a larger home to enable me to be a stay-at-home mom while our son was young. Buying a house we could afford on one income meant a fixer-upper for sure. With some major drywall replacement here and some minor electrical work there, the tiny house showed promise. Inside, we papered, carpeted, and painted it into a cozy nest. Outside, however, the clapboard siding was peeling and in dire need of paint.

We were wondering how we could afford that next step when a relative who worked for a local paint store called, offering us excess paint for the entire house for free. Nothing fancy, he warned, as he made arrangements to get the paint to us. We were delighted and grateful!

The exhausting process of scraping and sanding lasted a couple of weeks. During the day, I'd do what I could reach, and after coming home from work, my husband worked on the higher sections from his perch atop the ladder. The new paint seemed to glide on, shining and glowing, considerably renewing the tired cottage's curbside appeal.

We chose a bright contrasting trim color and got right to the final prep work. As we were scraping around the first window, we noticed that the glazing was so old, it had shriveled and pulled away from the pane. To our horror, we discovered that the only thing holding the glass in the window frame was inertia—a strong wind could have blown that window right in! Since our bed was directly beneath that window, it made the matter far more serious. Upon closer inspection, we found that all the windows were in various stages of decay.

Now what were we to do? This was more than a matter of sprucing up our little place; our family's safety was at stake. High winds were not unusual in our area, and with winter only a few months way, we faced a dilemma. We simply could not afford to replace the windows. We prayed for guidance, and we priced replacements, trusting that somehow God would provide.

As I called supply houses and home improvement centers, it became evident that the quaint charm of an older home also translates into expensive, hard-to-find replacement parts. I kept on looking for a better price. Later in the week, I chanced to pass a locally owned lumberyard. Hoping for a bargain, I stopped in to check. "Can you order those tall narrow windows? I have the measurements right here. Would you price them for me, please?"

As the manager's wife looked up the items, she chatted amicably with me and my son, who sat at her eye level in my backpack carrier. I told her about our little "dollhouse" and all the work we'd already done to fix it up. I'm sure I was oozing with pride and delight at our handiwork.

She flipped catalog pages and quickly found the windows, tapping the page as she read off the cost to me. Aghast, my face paled, and tears burned my eyes. I hurriedly turned to leave, embarrassed by the sudden welling of emotions within me. I mumbled my thanks for her trouble; we couldn't afford to order the windows just now. I asked myself if we would *ever* have that much money at once and wondered how we'd be able to order the windows at all. I adjusted the backpack for the walk home and handed my son some raisins to munch along the way. But when my hand rested on the doorknob, I stopped, turned back to her, and quietly asked, "Would you allow installment payments?"

"Not for this type of special order item." She shook her head. "It needs to be paid in full before we place the order. The unusual size makes them impossible to sell in the event of a default." From the look on her face, I could see that they'd been burned before.

"Oh." I scraped my shoe on the worn wooden floor. Digging in my pocket, I extracted my checkbook and gently persisted. "Look, here is my checkbook." I strode back to the counter and held it open for her to read. "See those payday deposits the first of every month? And the remaining balance? Each pay period there is exactly $16 left after the bills are paid. I will give you half of that *every* payday." I went on before she could say anything. "Honestly, we're good for it, I *promise*. And if any bonuses or overtime come our way, we'll pay more than the installment minimum. I will come in *every* payday and make a payment."

To this day I have no idea where my boldness came from. Her eyes searched mine; I returned her gaze steadily even though my heart was pounding. My son, usually wriggling around in the backpack, was still and silent. Was it wishful thinking, or did I see her face soften ever so slightly?

Without another word, she wrote up the order. As she asked for our address and made arrangements for delivery, a hint of a smile danced in her eyes.

"W-what do I have to sign?" I stammered.

"Nothing," she said. "Just show up like you promised, and don't make me sorry for this."

Show up I did. I made the first payment the day the windows were delivered. We so enjoyed the lovely, easy-to-open, easy-to-clean windows that let the sun in and kept the weather out! Throughout the summer and fall my son and I regularly walked the several blocks to the lumberyard. I chatted with the store personnel, and he waved at the manager if she was too busy to talk. They always seemed have a sucker or a little something to delight my toddler.

Whenever we could, we made extra payments in addition to the one promised each payday. Before we knew it, I was making the last payment. When I walked into the lumberyard office that day, the manager came out from behind the desk and gave me a hug, smiling hugely. "You know, if everyone was good to their word and made small but regular payments, this would *always* work. Thank you for your diligence. This has truly been a pleasure. You've restored our faith in humanity."

At that, I couldn't help but ask, "What made you give *me*, a total stranger, the credit?"

"Well, honestly, you have the most earnest face I've ever seen. I don't know why I did it, except that I just couldn't say no to the need in your eyes."

It seems the manager's faith was restored, and our needs were supplied. Once again, when a door was closed, God opened a window—in this case, quite literally!

—*Maryjo Faith Morgan*

 Fear Not

I had just put my two-year-old in his crib for a nap when the phone rang. It was my neighbor Alicia. "Did you see the news last night?" she asked me.

I hadn't watched the news since October, when coverage of the sniper attacks in Washington, D.C. made me afraid to buy groceries or fill my gas tank. "No, what happened?"

"The Office of Homeland Security announced the threat of a chemical attack. We need to buy plastic sheeting and duct tape to seal our windows and doors."

"Seal the entire house with duct tape?" I asked, wanting to get the instructions right.

"No, just one room," she said. "Preferably one with a bathroom. And be sure to stock the room with water, nonperishable food, and a radio, as it may be a while before you can come out."

"Where did you hear this? Tabloid news?" It sounded so surreal.

"It was on all the stations, even CNN."

Well, that confirmed it.

"Oh, and if you're going to get a gas mask, you better hurry," she added. "People are buying them by the dozen, and stores are selling out."

"I will," I said, though I wasn't sure where to get one. I made a note to check the wilderness store where I'd bought kerosene grills and canned meat for the Y2K crisis. I ended the conversation and called my husband at work.

"You need to go by Home Depot on your way home and get some plastic sheeting and duct tape," I said hurriedly. "We're under the threat of chemical warfare. We need to seal our windows and doors."

"I'm not stopping to buy any sheeting," he said, "and we have duct tape in the garage."

"But it's not enough," I whined, thinking of the two measly layers of tape left on our roll and all of the homes we would have to seal. There was my mother, who was retired on disability, and my grandmother, who was in her seventies and lived alone. And I couldn't forget my uncle, who was mentally ill, or my friends in apartments who didn't have ladders to reach windows on the second floor.

"Sorry, dear, I'm not stopping," my husband said. His voice was as calm as if I'd asked him to buy a loaf of French bread, rather than provisions to ensure our family's existence. "If the chemicals are that strong, duct tape won't stop them. Besides, who says we'll be at home when the chemicals hit? You're likely to be at the mall."

"But that's why we need the gas masks—"

"I have to go," he interrupted. "I'm late for a meeting."

"Engineer," I said with disgust, hanging up the phone. I collapsed on the couch and clicked on the television for news about the attack. I am just as capable as he is, I reasoned. I'll secure the house myself.

"Immunizations—are they lifesaving or deadly? News special at six," the announcer said. The screen showed a picture of a family in surgical masks, standing around a young boy in a hospital bed. I programmed the VCR to tape the broadcast, then flipped to channel five. "Identity theft—one woman's story," the anchor intoned.

I turned to channel eight. "What is growing in your vents that can kill you?"

Channel eleven. "How secure is your retirement money?"

Channel thirteen. "Have big companies polluted our water supply? Full story ahead."

Mind racing, I turned off the television, closed my eyes, and listened to my son's rhythmic breathing over the infant monitor. A truck roared past, and I heard him stir for a moment before whimpering softly and bursting into an all-out wail.

"Mo-o-m-m-my!"

I rushed to his room, lifted him from his crib, and held him tightly to my chest as his wails returned to whimpers. I felt the warmth of his tears as he hid his head in my neck.

"Everything's okay, sweetie," I whispered. "Mommy's here." I stroked his short, fuzzy hair and rocked him gently. He closed his eyes and sighed, once again at rest. He was still too young to know I did not have all the answers. Only I knew there was nothing I could do to keep him safe.

Fear not. I heard a voice, whispering in my subconscious.

Fear not. A little louder, quieting my anxious thoughts.

Fear not. It was my Father, stilling the storms of my heart.

Fear not for I am with you. (Isaiah 43:5)

"He is with me," I said aloud, calming myself. In the midst of my nightmare of worry, God came to the rescue, and I clung to his Word as my son was clinging to me.

At two years of age, there is little my son can control. He eats what I feed him, wears what I put on him, and goes where I take him. Though I am approaching thirty, I cannot control much more.

What do I have that my Father hasn't provided? What door can I enter that he hasn't opened? What danger will I face that can't be conquered by his power? If my son can rest securely in my incapable arms, then I, forever in the presence of an almighty God, should always be at peace.

I never did go out and buy that plastic sheeting, and to my husband's delight, I'm no longer asking for a bomb shelter. Crime, pollution, disease, warfare—I can't stop the list from getting longer, but I can control where I place my faith. In this world of many terrors, I'll seek shelter in my Father's shadow, and I'll dwell in his secret place (Psalm 91), a place where no illness, no snipers, no chemicals can reach.

"Everything's okay, sweetie," he whispers. "Father's here."

—C. Carletta Sanders

A Lesson in Benevolence

I hear it, feel it, and immediately wish that it's not happening. But it is—my tire has gone flat. Drawing a deep breath, I quickly strategize, evaluating my options. Steering to the right toward the curb won't obstruct traffic, I reason. So I ease the car onto the shoulder and begin looking for help.

On the sidewalk are hurrying pedestrians, some talking on cell phones, others deep in thought—all of them too preoccupied to notice my fate. On the road cars speed past with drivers rushing frantically to their varied destinations.

Silently I pray, "Father, send someone. *Anyone!*"

Momentarily I'm distracted by two familiar figures just a few feet away—a woman and a young child. The woman, dressed in an ankle-length jean skirt and faded yellow blouse, displays a homemade sign with crooked letters in bold black that spell "Homeless" followed by the words "Please help." The child, a little girl who looks to be about five, clings to the woman's skirt and holds a Raggedy Ann doll. They've been standing on this corner now for at least four weeks, collecting change in a tin can from pedestrians and passing motorists who happen to be stopped by the intersection's traffic light. I, too, have dropped change or an occasional dollar into the woman's can, reasoning, like so many others, that these two need help.

Then I remember that a man, lean and balding, with a similar sign hanging from a rope around his neck shares the same corner. But today he's missing, and despite my own troubles, I wonder for a moment where he might be. Soon honking horns disrupt my wandering thoughts and force me back to my present dilemma. Observing no available assistance, I walk to my car's trunk, hoping and praying that someone might stop.

"Need some help?" I hear over my shoulder.

Turning to my left, I see him—the man bearing the homeless sign. I look him over and try not to appear startled. I reflect on his daily request for help, which other people, including me, have selectively ignored. His tenor voice repeats the question, clearly the offer I've been waiting for.

I back away from the trunk and allow him to open it. It is an awkward moment, but I permit a weak "Thank you" to pass my lips.

A closer look at the man's features suggests that he is actually prematurely bald and much younger than I had always thought. He is nearly six feet tall with a considerably lean frame and has a limp. There are holes in the knees of his jeans and in his faded green T-shirt.

"I . . . I appreciate your help," I say, breaking the silence between us. He nods, and I wait for permission to continue. He never looks up from his work, so again I speak up, adding, "Thank you again for changing my tire." After more silence, I muster more courage. "I've seen you at this corner for a while." This time I wait, hoping he will say something—anything to indicate that he's heard me.

This time my wait is short and rewarded with a sour, "I've seen you too!" His tone suggests that more is coming, so I wait for an indictment to pass his lips. But when no such accusation surfaces, my thoughts shift, and I ask if he lives in a shelter.

This time he looks up, briefly catching my eye, and I think twice about what I've asked. This answer is even shorter than the last—a polite, "No, ma'am." After a seemingly long pause, he continues, "I lost my job more than six months ago, and due to a chain of bad luck, well, I—" he stutters—"well, I . . . I ended up on the streets."

"What kind of work do you, or did you do?" I ask.

He proudly responds, "I'm a mechanic."

"I take it you've been looking." I stoop to catch his eye as he continues to work.

"Yep, every day. But with no fixed address or phone, it makes it hard for folks to get back to you. Where they gonna call, if they want to hire you?"

He pauses as if deep in thought, then adds, "Folks that come through here every day probably think I can do better. But ma'am, I'm trying, I'm really trying."

He finishes changing the tire, pats his hands on his already dirty jeans, and closes the car's trunk.

I fish through my purse looking for a dollar or two, but instead I decide to empty my wallet and give him all its contents—$15.00.

He smiles, saying, "I'm not charging you."

"I know," I answer, "but I insist that you take the money." After much urging, he thrusts the bills into a pocket and starts to walk away.

I again say thanks but motion for him to wait while I ask one more question. "Why did you choose to help me, when I've rarely helped you?" He looks at me, and without batting an eye answers, "'Cause it's the right thing to do." With that, he walks back to his street corner, and I drive away, knowing that I'm not the same.

The next day, I see him. He smiles, and we talk while waiting for the light to turn green. Before leaving the intersection, I drop a dollar bill in his cup. He says thanks.

The following day I do the same, and the next day too. On week two of this new routine, I leave a bag of fruit and a sandwich. He again says thanks. This continues for another two months. Then one day he tells me that he has a job and will start the following day. I wish him well and see him no more. And again—I'm not the same.

Heavenly Father, thank you for the lesson you taught me through this man. Thank you for the opportunity to learn from him the true meaning of benevolence.

—Yvonne Curry Smallwood

Prayer for an Easy-Bake Oven

The whir of the electric beaters, the clouds of flour puffing into the air, the grainy feel of sugar beneath your fingernails, the smell of brownies in the oven, the first bite of still-warm chocolate after a Saturday afternoon in the kitchen . . .

In my eight-year-old mind, there was only one thing that could be better than baking cookies and brownies with my mom—doing it all by myself.

"Dear God," I whispered as I snuggled under layers of blankets, "please send me an Easy-Bake Oven for Christmas." Let other kids write to Santa. I knew someone much more important.

Then, as an added incentive for God to fulfill my request in between the more pressing issues of earthquakes and endangered dolphins, I added, "I promise to make treats for my whole family. All the time." I paused. Was that enough? Better be sure, I thought. "I'll let my friends play with it. Even Mark." It was doubtful my six-year-old brother would be even vaguely interested, but I was sure God would be impressed by my generosity. "Thank you in advance. Yours sincerely, Michelle."

At that point I had a pretty successful track record with prayer. I prayed that no one would kick the soccer ball in my direction during P.E., and no one did. (Of course, the fact that I constantly ran in the opposite direction of the ball may have been a factor.) I prayed that my mom would never find out that I secretly hid my Halloween candy in my room and ate it after I was in bed. That worked pretty well, until my dentist let it slip that I had seven cavities. Still, I reasoned, that wasn't God's fault. I just hadn't thought to include the dentist in my prayer. The key to successful prayer, I figured, was being specific.

I closed my eyes and pictured the Easy-Bake Oven: smooth white box, lavender and pink trim. On the TV commercials, the girls mixed up their own chocolatey batter and seconds later pulled out finished brownies in their own tiny pan. If that wasn't a miracle, I didn't know what was. If God wanted me to be happy (and didn't it say that some-where in the Bible?), then he would listen to my prayer. Getting me an Easy-Bake Oven was a small thing, I reasoned, an easy thing. Something relaxing and fun for God to do in between the heavy-duty miracles of saving lives and converting enemies into friends. There was no good reason that my prayer wouldn't be answered.

Except one. Which I didn't discover until Christmas morning.

"Why?" I asked my mom, blinking back the tears. "Why didn't I get an Easy-Bake Oven for Christmas?"

"If you want to cook something," my mom said, "just let me know, and I'll help you." She smiled encouragingly at me. "You can use the real, grown-up oven with me, not a little box with a light bulb."

"But I want to do it all by myself," I sniffed. My eyes and nose were running. Wasn't eight practically a grown-up?

My mom handed me a tissue. "I'm sorry, Michelle, but you're not old enough. It isn't safe. Someday, I promise, you'll be able to use the grown-up oven all by yourself, whenever you want." She hugged me. "And one day you'll have your very own kitchen, and you'll be able to make chocolate chip cookies whenever you want. Won't that be something?"

I nodded. My very own oven. That would be something, indeed.

It was twenty years later. "How am I going to pay back those student loans?" I moaned to a friend on the phone. As I talked, I paced the short length of the kitchen in my apartment. Half-empty takeout cartons, books, and papers cluttered the table. "What if I've made a big mistake?"

Two years earlier I had moved to another state for graduate school. Graduation was a few months away. A few requests for interviews had trickled in, but most of my carefully written cover letters and resumes were attracting form rejection letters.

My friend and I talked for a few more minutes, and then I hung up, feeling vaguely depressed. I had lost the stubborn faith I'd had as a child, the belief that if I prayed hard enough, my wishes would be granted without question. The older I got, the less I prayed. I told myself that I prayed less because I didn't want to bother God. Now that I was an adult, I knew he was busy with more important concerns. Intellectually, I knew my life was good, even blessed. I had enough to eat, clothes to wear, a decent place to live, many wonderful friends and family. Spiritually, I wasn't sure.

To take my mind off my problems, I'd taken to entering sweepstakes, paying special attention to those that awarded large cash prizes or fancy cars. I knew the odds against winning were enormous— my friends never let me forget it. Still, there was something satisfying about filling in three-by-five cards with my name and address, in between bites of another microwave dinner or fast-food meal.

The doorbell rang, interrupting my daydreams of driving a red Porsche to class.

I frowned. "Who could that be?" I looked out the peephole and saw a delivery man carrying a huge square box.

Curious, I signed for the box and dragged it inside. Each side of the heavy box was two or three feet wide. I slit the top open with a knife and pulled out a letter.

"Dear Winner," I read, "Congratulations on winning second prize in our sweepstakes . . . " I dropped the letter and started pulling out items, one by one. Two baby dolls that could wet their diapers after being fed, a Monopoly board game, a few toy trucks, a whole collection of computer games. Amazed, I kept pulling toys out of the box, gleefully thinking of which friend or family member would get each one as a present this year. Then I saw it at the bottom of the box—the pink and lavender lettering was unmistakable.

An Easy-Bake Oven. I swallowed and gently pulled it out, my hands shaking. I hadn't thought about this toy in years, probably not since the fourth or fifth grade. I had completely forgotten, but God had not. Turns out, he was listening all the time.

—*Michelle Mach*

Finding God in a Ladybug's Wings

Ever since my divorce from the father of my three young daughters, I'd felt disconnected from God, even though he'd been a part of my life for as long as I could remember. My relationship with him had been straightforward, just normal, like it was with my best friend, Lisa, my parents, or my sisters. In high school and college, through marriage and the births of my girls, I talked to him about everything: my hopes, dreams, disappointments, fears. Then my marriage crashed, and with it my belief that God truly cared about what happened to me.

I still prayed about the big, important things—like September 11th and Saddam Hussein and the destruction of the rainforests. But when it came to me, to my family and the events of our everyday world, I was silent. That is, until the afternoon my six-year-old daughter, Chloe, found a ladybug and brought her home to be our pet.

I'd told Chloe and her sisters, Zoe and Caroline, the rules about pets in our apartment complex: It can't bark, meow, neigh, moo, or slither. A fish would be okay, but only if they were willing to clean the bowl. That had been enough to deter them. Then one day Chloe wandered inside with a grubby hand curled into a fist and a wide smile on her face.

"Mommy, I've found us a pet," she declared proudly as she opened her hand to reveal a fat, red-and-black creature caught in her sweaty palm. I looked down at the tiny insect and forced myself not to laugh. I'd said we couldn't have a dog or cat—I'd never said anything about a ladybug.

"Her name is Ashley, Mama. Can we keep her?" my impetuous daughter implored, eyes wide and pleading. Her two sisters joined in the plea. I looked down at my three lovely girls and nodded my head, grinning. "Yes, I told them, you can keep your ladybug for a pet."

They went into action. First, a glass mason jar for Ashley's home. Zoe picked grass blades to put in the bottom of the jar. Caroline dripped water from a straw onto the grass so Ashley wouldn't get thirsty. And Chloe was the Mother Protector. Nobody was allowed to touch the precious pet; only looking was permitted.

All afternoon they carried that jar around, showing Ashley off to the neighbor kids. They talked to her, sang "The wheels on the bus go 'round and 'round. . ."

(Chloe's favorite song), and plotted out who would get to sleep with the jar in their room each night for the next week. I smiled, listening to them, as I browned meat and shredded cheese for tacos.

Suddenly Chloe burst into the kitchen with a worried frown on her face. "Something's wrong with Ashley, Mom," she said. "She's not moving."

I took a look for myself. Sure enough, Ashley did not appear to be thriving in our care. She lay perfectly still on a single blade of grass. I couldn't tell if she was alive or dead.

"Chloe," I said, gathering my young daughter close, "maybe Ashley misses her mama. Maybe she wants to go home. Maybe we should let her go." I watched as my sweet child raised dark brown eyes to mine, and I saw the tears threatening to fall. But I was caught off guard by the maturity in her voice when she finally spoke.

"You're right, Mommy," she said, her voice barely audible. "But do you think she'll ever come back? Do you think we'll ever see her again, and will she remember us?"

I hugged Chloe and whispered, "I don't know if she'll come back, honey. But I think every time we see a ladybug, we'll know it might be her. And we'll know that, while she was here, we loved her."

Chloe nodded, trying not to cry, and together we went outside and carefully lifted Ashley out of the mason jar. We set her down on a piece of grass, and nothing happened for a long moment. Suddenly, as abruptly as she'd entered our life, Ashley was gone... lifting tiny wings to fly away.

That night, as I watched my daughters sleeping in their beds, I had a talk with God. I told him I was sorry that I had been distant and that I missed him. I talked to him about Ashley the ladybug and how my daughters were always teaching me to find miracles in ordinary things: that ladybugs can be pets, that rocks can be diamonds, that dew on the grass can be magic drink for invisible leprechauns hiding under mushrooms. "They believe it all, Lord," I told him, "and they don't need anyone else to convince them."

I told him that if he could help a six-year-old let a beloved ladybug go, maybe he could help a forty-year-old mother let go of a few things too—like foolish pride and a bitter spirit.

"I love you, God," I prayed that night, "and I thank you for showing up on a ladybug's wings."

—*Donna Surgenor Reames*

God Cares about Christmas

I hated Chicago! Oh yes, I had said that I would be willing to live in the city for the three years it would take my husband to complete his schooling at Moody Bible Institute. After all, God had called him into ministry. Then God had made it clear that Dan needed to obtain his Bible education at Moody. And how could one argue with God?

So, that fall Dan and I and our two children moved to Chicago from our small town in Ohio. On the outside, I was the picture of a submissive wife. But on the inside, I went kicking and screaming every inch of the way.

When our daughter was born, Dan and I had made the decision that I would be a stay-at-home mom. Then our son came along twenty-two months later, and we were sure that we had made the right decision. Now the children were six and four. Even though the extra income would have helped with the high cost of living in Chicago, we were still committed to my being at home. With Dan working part-time on campus, we were making out okay. Just okay . . . no extras!

But then came the Christmas season. I have been an absolute nut over Christmas for as long as I can remember. I love the carols on the radio, the cookie baking, the tree, and the decorations. I love the pageants at church, Santa Claus, even shopping. I've always loved to find just the right gift for everyone on our list.

That was probably why there was such trepidation in Dan's voice one evening in late November when, after the kids were put to bed, he said, "Honey, we need to talk about Christmas."

I said, "Sure. I have already been planning what we will get for our parents and . . . " Then I saw his face. His eyes were full of tears. "Danny, what is it?" I asked.

Slowly he pulled his billfold out of his pocket. Shaking his head, he said, "There just isn't any money. I have tried to save money from each paycheck so we could buy gifts. This is it." His hand shook as he presented me with ten dollars.

I just stared at him and choked, "You've got to be kidding! That won't even buy a decent toy for the kids!"

"I know," he mumbled, looking even more dejected. "I'm so sorry. But it's taking more for groceries than we anticipated, and our budget is…" His voice trailed off as he saw the tears begin to flow down my cheeks. He reached to pull me into his arms, but I pushed him away.

"This isn't fair!" I burst out. "God called you into ministry. God called you to come to Moody. And now he doesn't even provide us with enough money to celebrate the birth of his son the way I want to!" I knew my words didn't make sense, but I went on. "There has to be a way. I know—we can call our parents."

Dan immediately said no to that idea. "Sure, if they knew how strapped we were financially, they would help. But I feel positive that we should not ask anyone in our families for help. I don't want people to pity us. God has promised to take care of us," he insisted.

"Well then—why isn't he doing it?" I exploded. "I gave up so much to move here. Don't tell me I have to give up Christmas too!"

My ever-gentle husband just pulled me into his arms and let me cry. After the tears had subsided, he said, "We won't give up Christmas. It just won't be exactly the same kind of Christmas we have had in the past. I think with $10 you can find a nice doll for Sonya and a truck for Kyer. I'll keep the kids tomorrow after school, and you can go shopping at that thrift store on Belmont. You'll feel better then."

"But what about us?" I whimpered.

"I don't think we should plan on getting each other anything this year," he replied.

We prayed together before going to bed. As tears slid down my cheeks, Dan prayed that God would remind us of the true meaning of Christmas. I prayed that God would help me to find bargains and figure out a way to make Christmas something like it had always been. With still-heavy hearts, we went to bed.

The next day dawned bright and crisp. The sky was the kind of blue that almost hurts your eyes, and as always in Chicago, there was a stiff wind. I tried to be happy as I bundled the kids for the three-block walk to Sonya's school. As Kyer and I walked back to our apartment after dropping Sonya off, I noticed he was limping slightly. It didn't take long to discover the reason. After returning home, I examined his foot and found a big hole worn through the sole of his shoe. Kyer laughed and said he'd been meaning to tell me about it. I instructed him to put on his slippers, and he trotted off happily to find them. In a few minutes, I could hear him digging through his toy box, so I knew he wouldn't see me dissolve into tears.

I wrestled with God big-time that morning. "Now we have to buy shoes! You must really not care about us. I can't believe we gave up everything to move up here so that we can serve you and . . ." My haranguing went on and on.

That afternoon Kyer was looking out his bedroom window, which had a clear view of the street. "Mailman, Mommy!" he shouted. I told him to wait while I got the key to the box and trudged down the steps.

"Anything for me?" he eagerly asked upon my return.

Wanting to see him smile, I said, "I'm pretty sure these are Christmas cards. Do you want to open them?"

While he was inspecting the cards and trying to read the senders' names, I opened the rest of our mail. There was a telephone bill that would make Dan see red and a flyer for a sale at Sears. Then I opened a long envelope with type on the front and no return address.

As I unfolded the single typewritten page, a piece of paper fell to the floor. I was so intent on learning who had sent the letter, I ignored it. I started to smile when I saw the letter was from my cousin Suzie. She had never written to us before. We had been close as children but had drifted apart a bit. She got married and had four daughters in three years. Her twins were Sonya's age, and her youngest was Kyer's. Just before we moved to Chicago, our families had gotten together a couple of times, but we'd lived here since August, and this was our first letter from her.

Kyer wandered back toward me and picked up the slip of paper. "What is this?" he asked.

By then, I had read only the first line of the letter, which said, "We just want you guys to have this for Christmas." The slip of paper was a check for $100.

"Don't cry, Mommy," my son begged.

Pulling him into my arms, I said, "It's okay, honey. These are happy tears. You see, God just proved to me all over again that he wants us to be here so Daddy can study to be a pastor."

Of course, Kyer didn't really understand, so I called Dan at his part-time job.

"Hi, babe," he said, sounding very chipper. "I was just getting ready to call you."

Interrupting him, I said, "Danny, listen! You are never going to believe this." My words came out in a breathless rush. "Kyer was limping on the way home from school, and he has a hole in his shoe, and we're going to have to spend the $10 on shoes for him, and I was so mad at God, but then the mail came, and Suzie sent us a check for $100, and now we can have Christmas!" He could hear the tears in my voice, but he understood what kind of tears they were. I went on to apologize for my behavior the prior evening.

He just let me babble. Finally I stopped to take a breath. That's when Dan got a chance to explain why he was about to call. When he got to work that afternoon, there was an envelope on his desk. Inside was a handwritten letter from the much older lady who worked there in the mornings while he was in class. The letter said:

> *Dear Dan,*
>
> *I can remember when my children were small, and money was tight. It always seemed like right at Christmastime they would need shoes. So, if that happens to be true in your home right now, please take this $40 and buy each of your children a pair of shoes. If not, use it however you want. No need to even thank me. God told me to give you this money. Give my love to your wife. May God bless you as you prepare to serve Him.*
>
> *Your friend,*
> *Lucy*

Needless to say, we had Christmas that year—perhaps one of our biggest and best! I know for sure it was the most appreciated Christmas in my life up to that point. Since then, I have learned Christmas is not all about the gifts we give or receive. In fact, we've cut back on the number and cost of our presents. But God knew that at that time in my life I needed to celebrate the birth of his son in the same manner I always had. Suzie and Lucy both gave us gifts we will never forget, but I know the idea for those gifts came from God.

—Raelene Phillips

A Call for Help

"Go! Call the fire department!" my husband, Tom, half yelled, half coughed as flames licked at his boots.

We thought we could control it, thought we had time to get it stopped, but the fire was raging now and threatening not only the mobile home we kept as a rental property but the neighbor's big barn as well.

My eyes smarted, and my throat burned as I left Tom there to try to keep the flames from swallowing our tenants' home.

I ran to our house and made the call. The dispatcher at our small local firehouse said, "Oh, yes. Out on Musgrove? We've already gotten a call, and the trucks are on the way."

Some neighbor must have seen our dilemma.

I quickly checked the baby in the playpen, thankful that she was playing quietly and entertaining herself, then I ran back out to assist my husband until help arrived.

We'd started this dumb fire ourselves. There was an untilled area behind the mobile home that extended all the way through the ditch to the road. It had become overgrown with burdock, and we wanted to clean it out.

It was the perfect time in March, after the snow was gone but before the new spring growth had started. Earlier that day, there had been only a light breeze. Still, we took time to rake the dried grass and weeds away from the telephone pole and the one tree in the area.

Then I'd taken the baby inside to change her and get her settled for a nap. While I was in the house, Tom decided to start the fire. A city boy, he didn't realize we needed to start at the top, away from the wind, and burn toward the wind and the ditch. He'd lit several small fires in the ditch, and with all the fuel and the upward slope, the fire had taken off dramatically. When I stepped outside, I could see from the house that the flames were huge.

"Oh, Lord," I said as I broke into a run.

As a kid, I'd been present many times when Dad burned off the bean fields after harvest. I knew the wind had to be considered and worked with, or things could easily get out of hand.

"Why did you start down there? Man, we could be in trouble." I grabbed the shovel and started dragging dead grass and debris away from the fence behind the mobile home.

"I figured it would be quicker this way," was all he said.

"You're right about that," I answered.

It wasn't long at all before Tom was sending me in to call the fire department.

When I returned two minutes later, I was stunned at the raging inferno that had erupted during my absence. I noticed our neighbor girl, Marilyn, who sometimes babysat for us, in her yard and called to her for help. She grabbed a rake and came running.

For the next several frightening moments, we ran back and forth at the leading edge of the blaze, trying to stop the fire using a combination of shovel, rake, and a piece of old carpet which Tom used to try to smother the flames. Just when we got one area beat back, another one erupted. Some places were just too hot to get in there and try to fight it.

There was a woven wire fence only a few feet behind the mobile home, and our tenants, who were away for the weekend, had surrounded the base of the mobile home with straw bales for added insulation during the winter. Now the flames came licking and crawling toward that fence and the straw. I scraped and beat with renewed urgency, trying to keep the fire from reaching that fencerow.

I was beginning to choke and gag from all the smoke. The saliva in my mouth had become thick and acrid. My eyes and nose flowed from the stinging air.

As the flames began to work the fencerow, my heart sank. "Where are the firemen?" I cried.

The openings in the fence were too small to get the shovel through, and the fence was too high to reach over. I felt a sense of desperation as I continued to fight.

I could feel myself growing weaker. I was exhausted and couldn't get a good breath. We were all wheezing and coughing as we struggled to contain the fire. I leaned on the shovel handle as the flames continued to reach through to the other side of the fence. One of the straw bales caught fire. Tom jumped the fence, grabbed it, and with a growl threw it as far as he could toward the yard.

As I stood still, my mind quieted, and I remembered our Sunday school class that week in which we'd been studying the sixth chapter of Ephesians and the armor of God. *"After having done all, stand. Stand therefore."* The words from the end of verse 13 and the beginning of verse 14 reverberated in my mind. Faith rose up in me, and I raised my voice in prayer.

"Lord God, we have done all we can do here. We are beat. All we can do is stand. We give this fire to You, Father. It's Your fire now. Send angels. Send rain. Stop the wind. Do something. But please put the fire out. I ask it in Jesus' name, amen."

Tom and Marilyn both looked at me with raised eyebrows.

I somehow had such confidence. I fully expected rain to fall or the wind to cease, but that's not what happened. Instead, the wind seemed to pick up, and it was blowing right toward the mobile home.

But, remarkably, as we stood there panting for air, the flames began to shrink in size and intensity. They just diminished before our eyes, even though the wind gusted and there was all kinds of fuel to feed the fire. It was one of those moments when your brain tells you that your eyes cannot be seeing what they are seeing, and yet you see it.

From the time I said "Amen," the fire did not progress another foot, and within five minutes the whole thing was out. The tears from my eyes changed from pain to joy as I realized I was witnessing a miracle.

We went dutifully along the fifty-foot fire line to tamp out any remaining sparks, but there were none. All that dead, dry fuel next to the charred ground seemed totally incongruous, but there it was.

Only later did we learn that there was another grass fire that afternoon on Musgrove, and the dispatcher had made the mistake of not taking my information, assuming it was a repeat call. We also learned that there was another grass fire nearby that had gotten out of hand and had burned a mobile home to the ground. It was a very humbling and sober thing to hear.

When word got back to the fire chief about the mix-up, he and a couple of volunteer firemen came to our home to apologize. We took them out behind the mobile home and showed them how close we'd come to serious property damage and loss. Of course, we had to tell them how the fire went out. The chief walked quietly along the fire line, seeing that the fuel was all right there and had not been beaten or dug or wet.

There were tears in his eyes as he shook his head and said, "Well, it must be as you say, a miracle. There is no other explanation. God put out this fire."

—*Diane Meredith Vogel*

Stretching My Prayer Muscle

I awoke tired again. My eyes felt dry and puffy, as if I'd just cried my heart out. There was the pain of a sinus headache behind my eyes. The day ahead was full of things to do, but they all seemed pointless. What was the use? Did I ever really accomplish anything? Did any of the tasks on my to-do list really help anyone? I felt as if everything I did was useless. I'd come to recognize this dull sadness as depression. It had been plaguing me off and on lately.

"What's wrong?" my husband, Phil, asked as I dragged myself around that morning.

"I'm just tired," I replied.

Whatever the cause, I didn't want to feel this heaviness in my emotions and spirit. To avoid the feelings of hopelessness, I'd sometimes escape by watching TV. Phil definitely did not need to hear my grousing about feeling depressed when he had so many other things on his mind.

What could I do to bring back the joy? I'd learned some years ago that praising God could help. I also knew that listening to my favorite Christian praise music could help.

Today, though, none of my "fixes" worked; it was going to be one of those depression days. To make matters worse, I had to go to the Y to exercise. I'd already missed two weeks, what with the Thanksgiving holiday taking a bite out of my time. It was much easier to say, "Next week I'll get back to exercising," but I'd continue to put it off.

My friend Pat and I have been walking together every week for over twenty years. Two years ago we decided we needed to build up our strength, too, and a good way to do that was to join the Y. We each needed the other to push us into the program; but once we started, we were committed. Making a financial commitment to the program also helped us make the most of the facility. Now, though, Pat and I went at different times. We still shared how hard it was to face those machines twice a week, even though they would keep us healthy in our old age.

Well, today I had to push myself to go to the Y. Where was the joy I remembered having? I needed that joy that bubbles up and keeps me smiling. Right now it felt like my feet were dragging, along with my spirit.

The Y looked the same as always, its walls lined with Nautilus machines and weights. I had successfully avoided them these past two weeks, but today the machines beckoned me. Sometimes I vary the order in which I work on them. First, the compound row for my arms. It's the hardest, so I like to get it over with first. Then I select the weights for my biceps and triceps. I'm too short to use the regular Nautilus machines, so the free weights are a good substitute. When my arms get tired, I switch to the legs: leg extension, leg curl. With my spirit depressed and my listless body facing the dreaded machines, I wondered how I'd get through the long forty-five minutes it takes me to get through my program.

Then I remembered something I'd tried once before—prayer! I had just come from visiting friends in a local nursing home. Thoughts of them weighed heavily on my heart. Charlie was there rehabilitating from a hernia operation. He wanted to be well enough to go to Florida in two weeks to be with his sister for Christmas. Verna was a permanent resident of the home, the mother of a friend of mine. She was always happy to see me come. Mildred, who used to come and entertain the residents, was now herself a permanent resident of the nursing home. I never seemed to have (or take) the time to pray for these folks when I was busy around home or at church. Maybe, I thought, I should try lifting them up as I exercised.

At the first machine, I prayed "Lord, Charlie needs your healing touch. Please heal him." Then I'd start, "one, Charlie," "two, Charlie," "three, Charlie," etc., until I'd done the required series of moves on that machine. At the next machine, I lifted up Verna in the same way. Then Mildred, and, on the next machine, I lifted up my brother-in-law Jerry, who was having heart problems. At the next, our new pastor, and the next, her husband, who was dying of cancer.

As I prayed through my sets on the series of machines, there came a point when I actually felt something in my spirit shift. I was surprised by the fact that I was done with the exercises in what seemed like no time at all. The change, though, was more than the quick passing of time. The sadness that had burdened me was gone, and my heart felt lighter. I felt like smiling, and some of the joy began to return to my heavy soul. What seemed so strange was that the change really *felt* like a shift, as if I had been functioning on one level, and somewhere in my spirit I shifted to another level that carried the joy of the Lord. I realized that in praying for these people in my life, I was not only taking the focus off my sadness but was also carrying out God's will by interceding for those around me.

When I came to the stretches at the end of my lifting routine, I included myself in my prayers. "Lord, take my depression, help me to sleep, heal my reflux problem," etc.

My visit to the Y that day not only stretched my muscles but also my faith. I had needed to put more time into spirit stretching through intercessory prayer, and now I knew a great place to do that. My visits to the Y would no longer be a trial in perseverance. I looked forward to them as an opportunity to stretch my faith and as a time for prayer. God never said we couldn't pray and count repetitions at the same time! He knows our hearts and can hear right through the counting.

—*Laurie Perkins*

Dousing the Devil's Darts

I t hurts when bubbles burst. My bubble had insulated me for over four years. It was safe. Comfortable. But, as bubbles tend to do, mine burst without warning one evening in January.

It had been a typical day. I negotiated peace treaties, fed the hungry, and clothed the naked. In other words, I mothered three preschool children. My husband, Wes, arrived home as I was adding the finishing touches to dinner. He came up behind me, hugged me tight, and uttered the words that stuck the pin in my bubble: "My position at the university has been cut."

Shock numbed my brain. I turned to face him and asked inanely, "Are you sure?" He looked at me like I was crazy, but in my anesthetized state, I couldn't think of anything more intelligent to say.

The kids giggled and played in the next room, blissfully ignorant that their parents had just encountered a severe threat to their livelihood. On May 31st the paychecks would cease. Sure, the economy had been declining over the last few years, but that was no excuse. This could not be happening to us!

The following morning, I awoke still in a state of horrified disbelief. Throughout the day, I found myself obsessing about our misfortune. Stuck in a rut of negative thinking, I was bowled over by a wave of panic. What would we do? Would we have to move? Leaving our home was not an option I wished to consider.

I made myself sit down and take several deep breaths. Time for some reminders: *I believe in my husband's ability to provide for our family; more importantly, I believe in God's grace and mercy.* My heart rate slowed as encouraging Scriptures ran through my mind. "Do not worry about tomorrow." "Cast your anxiety on him because he cares for you." Finally, I began to pray.

Naturally, requests for employment dominated my prayer life. Although I trusted God to take care of us, I still felt the occasional jab of a dart piercing my heart. Satan relentlessly hurled flaming arrows of stress, worry, doubt, and fear at me. My shield of faith must have wavered at times, because the burn of those fiery darts singed my soul more than once.

Horrible fates flashed before my eyes. Unemployment. Welfare. Homelessness. Tension spread through me like a disease. I snapped at my kids. I grouched at my husband. My neck and back ached. A dark cloud of what-ifs hung over my spirit, obscuring life's beauty and joy. It wasn't long before my children began exhibiting similar symptoms. That's when I knew I had to make a change before all of us became bogged down in the mire of my anxiety.

Prayer became my lifeline. The persistent widow described by Jesus in Luke 18 served as my model. Dozens of times during the day, my spirit cried out, "Please help us find work. Please let us keep our home. Protect us, and help me to trust you more."

January melted into February, but with no noticeable thaw in the job market. One evening after the kids were in bed, Wes and I sat in his office going over our financial records. Scrolling through the computer spreadsheet that summarized our expenses, Wes spoke hesitatingly.

"We've barely scraped by the last few months, and I'm afraid that any new job I may find will force me to take a pay cut. I know you don't want to hear this, but you need to consider going back to work. If we had two full-time salaries, we could afford to keep the house."

No! Inside, my heart screamed in denial, but my mind recognized the truth of his words. Just when I thought I had my stress under control, Satan wound up and fired his rounds at me again:

The Dart of Sadness: I love being a stay-at-home mom. I can't leave my babies. My youngest is only eleven months old. The idea of going back to work breaks my heart.

The Dart of Anger: I better find the perfect job, because there is no way I'm leaving my kids for a monotonous daily grind.

The Dart of Fear: My master's degree in psychology has lain dormant for over five years. Who would want to hire me?

Perceiving the danger of these thoughts, I returned to my knees to pray. God patiently listened while I begged for strength, patience, and a dose of his holy peace powerful enough to banish these ungodly worries. I clung to his promises to "give good gifts to those who ask him" and "that in all things God works for the good of those who love him."

God's spirit of peace flooded my soul and repaired the dart holes in my heart. God would never leave me or forsake me. Even if my worst imaginings came to pass, and we ended up unemployed and homeless, God would remain with us, watching over our family and giving us strength to endure. I finally realized that the terrifying Monster of the Unknown, which had planted these scenarios in my head, was nothing more than a giant shadow projected on a wall by a tiny, insignificant bug. As I mentally squashed that bug, I vowed to trust God and wait.

A career counseling position opened at the university, and the head of the department just happened to be a friend of mine from graduate school. If anyone would give me a job in my field of study, it would be this man. He did grant me an interview, but the position went to another applicant.

Disappointment and frustration threatened, but God's voice whispered, "Trust me."

February passed. No job offers. We asked church and family members to pray on our behalf.

March passed. No job offers. We asked our friends and acquaintances to pray.

April passed. Still no job offers. We began asking strangers to pray.

The end of May arrived all too quickly. Time had run out, but God's voice grew stronger: "Trust me."

I looked at the calendar on the kitchen wall. Friday, May 31, loomed large at the end of the week. Worry butterflies fluttered in my stomach off and on during the next few days, but God's peace continually returned to still them. On Thursday the phone rang. The university had approved a new position in another department, and they wanted Wes to start on Monday. Hallelujah!

"But wait," God seemed to say, "There's more."

Friday morning, my friend in the career counseling office offered me a job as testing coordinator. I danced around my room in joyous celebration!

God truly knows how to give good gifts to his children. When my "happy dance" ended, and my spirit calmed, I once again approached the throne of grace to thank the one who had answered our prayers and healed my soul.

> *Do not be anxious about anything, but in everything, by prayer and petition, with thanksgiving, present your requests to God. And the peace of God, which transcends all understanding, will guard your hearts and your minds in Christ Jesus. (Philippians 4:6-7)*

—Karen Witemeyer

God's Perfect Timing

O ne winter evening, my husband, John, announced that his coworkers, Ranjan and Suzanne, had invited us to join them for a week of backpacking in Colorado's Weminuche Wilderness the coming summer.

"Have fun," I said. Hauling a forty-pound pack was not my idea of a vacation.

"Come on, Deb," John prodded. "You can do it. You've done weekend trips. This is just a little longer."

"A little?" I balked. "It's seven days!"

John adopted what he thought was a subtler strategy. "Think how much you'll grow from the experience."

Over the next few days, my husband encouraged and affirmed, kidded and cajoled. I finally conceded, on one condition: that our wilderness week be followed by an equal amount of time exploring New Mexico via bed and breakfast inns, fine dining, and art galleries.

Summer rolled around, and before I knew it, so did the time for our backpacking "vacation." The trip began with a series of anxiety-provoking events, including nearly missing the train that deposited us in the wilderness. While the others started off, I stood staring after it, as my link to civilization pulled away, gears grinding, smoke billowing. "Wait!" I wanted to scream. "I've made a mistake!"

That first day, I fought exhaustion and despair. An abundance of snow on higher trails forced us to scrap our plan of a seven-day circuit hike and settle for day hikes from a base camp. I tried to hide my relief.

But I could not hide my feelings on our next excursion. Descending down a precipitous path on legs wobbly from fatigue, I was convinced a giant hand would pluck me off the mountain and fling me to my death. From then on, I stuck close to camp while the more courageous ventured further. Guilt over "copping out" weighted me down. On the fifth day, John and Suzanne convinced me to join them on a short jaunt. Ranjan remained at camp resting a sore back. Drizzle turned to downpour that afternoon, and the three of us took refuge under a cluster of pines. While Suzanne and John chatted, I fantasized about a warm bed, a hot shower, and a decent meal. After the rain let up, we started off. Suzanne led while I trailed behind, cautiously plotting my course. Suddenly I heard a shout.

"Hey! Wait up!"

I spun around and froze. It had been days since I'd heard a stranger's voice, much less a frantic call. Searching the steep slope above me, I spotted a flash of red.

"Do you have a cell phone?" hollered a hiker, barreling down the zigzag path. "Someone's hurt!"

"Hurt?" I thought. "Out here?"

John called back, "No. What happened?"

"This guy fell off Mount Eolus. Says he fell on Thursday."

"Thursday?" I sputtered. "Two days ago?"

"Yup," said the hiker, catching up. "Me and my buddies were coming back from Sunlight Peak. We found an abandoned pack. Knew something was wrong. We searched and found the guy under a ledge."

I glanced up at the 14,000-foot peaks, anxiety pricking my chest.

"How bad's he hurt?" asked Suzanne.

"Pretty bad. He kinda goes in and out. I gotta find a cell, or this guy's a goner." The man took off, bounding down the trail like a mountain goat.

"Good luck!" I called. My words felt futile. But what could I do?

Further down the trail, we spotted a turquoise one-man tent on a rock ledge by some scrubby pines. A toothbrush tethered to a tree was the only evidence that the site had been inhabited. Could this be the injured hiker's campsite? While John and Suzanne waited, I scrambled inside, hunting for clues.

If I could just find a name, I thought, my throat tight and dry. Maybe that'd help.

A down sleeping bag and ragged-edged paperback were swept to one side. I spotted a nylon sack at the foot of the tent, crawled toward it, and began digging through dirty clothes.

What am I doing? A mixture of guilt and disgust washed over me.

Suddenly, my fingers hit on crumpled paper. I whisked it out, scanned it, and gasped.

"What'd you find?" called John.

"His name's Kurt!" I shouted. "Kurt Franz! He came in by train on Wednesday!"

Suzanne peered into the tent. "It's gotta be the injured guy. It all fits. His sleeping bag's here, John found his food sack. This guy was coming back."

"We have to tell Ranjan," I said, feeling like a detective who'd solved a mystery.

Returning to camp, Ranjan jolted me back to reality. "Deborah, where's the first-aid kit?" he demanded. "That hiker already came back through. He found a ranger with a cell, but we're too far out for it to work. They're hiking back to the tracks." Ranjan stuffed his sleeping bag into his pack. "I'm going up to help the injured guy."

"I'll go with you," said Suzanne.

My stomach clenched.

Ranjan and Suzanne could make the climb in an hour. I knew better than to volunteer. For once, I was grateful for Suzanne's stamina—instead of jealous.

"Even if someone gets to a cell, how will a helicopter ever find Kurt?" I asked.

Ranjan hoisted up his backpack, snapping the waist belt together. "I gave the guys the GPS coordinates. I had them from the other day."

"Thank God," I whispered.

After Ranjan and Suzanne left, John lit our tiny gas stove so we could prepare dinner. As it sputtered and choked, trying to coax water to boil, we sat silently. Anxiety hovered over us, and we felt uncertain and afraid. God, we need you, I prayed. Be up on that peak.

I forced dinner down, guilt-ridden that I was sitting at camp while our friends were trying to save someone's life.

It was nearly dark when Suzanne returned. "We were right," she said, setting down her pack. "It was Kurt. We cleaned a gash on his head and some other cuts. Something's really wrong with his left foot. It's twisted weird. Ranjan and two other guys are staying overnight with him. They'll need more supplies in the morning. I've gotta go back up at five. John, would you go with me?"

My husband nodded. Fear sparked inside of me. What if something happened to John, too?

I'd just fallen asleep when Suzanne's husky voice awoke us the next morning. I fetched John's backpack and poles, then watched him and Suzanne disappear into the darkness. Crawling back into the cozy cocoon of my sleeping bag, I thought, you did it again, Deb. You took the easy way out.

I dozed fitfully, prayers fluttering in and out of my mind. After waking, I popped a handful of dried cereal into my mouth. How could I be eating? We had so little food left.

I busied myself with chores: draping unzipped sleeping bags over boulders, scrubbing socks in the stream. But my mind was like a magnet snapping back to the injured hiker. Who was Kurt? Was he married? Did he have kids? I shuddered, realizing that I knew more about his present state than his family did.

Midmorning, I glanced at the gray sky and gulped. A storm was brewing. Brushing my teeth for the third time, I blinked back tears as I watched foamy spit cling to clusters of pine needles.

There was nothing I could do.

Nothing.

"God," I prayed, "save Kurt."

Suddenly, a faint murmur melded into the mountain stillness. I cocked my head. A quiet hum expanded in the air. With a yelp, I rushed to the river and scanned the sky. A helicopter buzzed in from the east like a metal dragonfly.

"Thank you, thank you!" I shouted, flinging my toothbrush. Retrieving it, I gazed back at the mountaintops.

Stillness.

Quiet.

"Please," I begged, feeling like I'd vomit. "Bring it back."

I crumpled to the ground, eyes pinned on the peaks. Time froze. Icy fingers crawled up my scalp.

Then something swooped. Tears cascaded down my cheeks as I watched the helicopter circle, hover, and land.

Two days later I read the lead in *The Durango Herald*: "A lone climber was rescued Sunday morning and remains in serious condition after a fall rendered him helpless on a mountainside for three days." I continued to pray for Kurt as John and I headed to New Mexico. Ranjan called to report that he and Suzanne had visited Kurt in a Denver hospital before heading to the airport. Kurt was in good spirits and grateful for the team that helped him survive. Before this experience, Kurt had apparently neglected certain relationships with loved ones and had lost sight of the things that are really important. But now he was eager to reevaluate his priorities and make the most of his new lease on life. His girlfriend summed it up best: "God didn't save Kurt on that mountain; he threw him there to wake him up."

I woke up on that mountain, too. God had given each of us a job to do, and my role of providing prayer and support had been just as important as giving Kurt direct care. God had ensured Kurt's survival by placing us exactly where he needed us. There are no accidents. Only God's perfect timing.

—Deborah M. Ritz

Not Your Average Joe (or Jane)

I was browsing through a bookstore next to two women engaged in a conversation about books they would like to read.

"I just love romance, don't you?" said one of them.

"Yes," said the other woman, "but I'm more interested in reading something historical, like *Gone with the Wind*." Then she turned to me and asked, "What would you like to read?"

"Probably *The Lord of the Rings*," I said. "It was recommended to me in college."

Their jaws dropped. Indignant, one of the women asked "That's it? You wouldn't want to read something more romantic?"

"No, that bores me," I said.

They continued their conversation without me, while I wandered away and wondered, not for the first time, why I couldn't be more like other women.

On the surface I look like a normal woman, but if you talk to me even for a short time, you will see that I am different. In school I was more of a math and science person than an English and history person. As I grew up, I found that I got along with guys better than girls because my interests are more like theirs. I like reading science fiction and fantasy. I enjoy college football. I would rather get outside and do things like hiking, boating, or fishing than sit inside and watch talk shows or soap operas. In fact, I find many traditionally female interests, like shopping, sewing, decorating, and cooking to be dull if not aggravating.

I suppose this could be because men have always had a powerful influence on my life. My mother and maternal grandmother were wonderful people and taught me many invaluable lessons, but when it came to social development, the men in my family definitely had a strong influence. My father spent a great deal of time with me, especially helping me with my schoolwork. He was determined that I would not be a girl who couldn't do math, and he went to great efforts to make sure that I excelled in this area. I also have a brother six years my senior, and he definitely shaped me in those critical early years of socialization. I often joke with my parents that having an older brother served two purposes—he kept me from being overly feminine, and he raised my IQ by at least ten points. I always had to think about whether his "brilliant ideas" would make us millions or get us both sent to our rooms. The fact that my best friend in school had two brothers didn't help either—in fact, it was probably why we had so much in common.

Of course, despite all the male influences on my life, I'm not totally devoid of feminine characteristics. I have long hair, I never go out without makeup, and I wear nice dresses for church, work, and special occasions. I can even be a proper lady when the occasion calls for it. But I am more comfortable in jeans and hiking boots than panty hose and high heels any day! (Incidentally, I did read *The Lord of the Rings*, and I loved it. Now that I've read it, I can't help but wonder if those two women in the bookstore that day have any idea of what they are missing!)

Although genetic makeup and environmental influences may explain a little of why I am the way I am, the truth is that I am what God made me. I believe that each of us has been placed in this world for a purpose, and God made us the unique individual we are in order to serve that purpose. It is our differences that make us valuable not only to God but to the world as well.

But we live in a world that demands conformity, so we have a tendency to hide our differences from other people. This is where I ran into problems with my own individuality. I could see how my differences made me unique, but it was hard to see how God could use such an atypical person. How could I help or serve people if they didn't understand me? The incident with the two women in the bookstore was a perfect example of how people reject and fear what they don't understand. But instead of letting it make me feel bad, I decided it was time that I came to terms with my individuality.

I came across a gem of advice in Paul's first letter to the Corinthians, where he explains his transition from blasphemer to apostle. Instead of beating himself up over his former actions, Paul tells the Corinthians that "by the grace of God I am what I am, and his grace toward me was not in vain" (1 Corinthians 15:10). I admire Paul's attitude. Instead of being held back by who he was, Paul simply accepted God's forgiveness and accepted himself as God had made him.

This verse opened my eyes to a problem with humanity in general. I don't believe there has ever been a person who did not suffer from fears of inadequacy. It is human nature to focus more on what is wrong than on what is right. The pressure to conform is especially hard on women, even more so in an age where we are expected to do more than women in generations past. I feel the pressure to keep my life in perfect order every day. We are expected to be loving wives, perfect housekeepers, and caring children of our aging parents, and motivated employees at our jobs. Sometimes it seems there just aren't enough hours in the day to work eight hours at a job, put a meal on the table, grocery shop, clean the dishes, do the laundry, tidy up the house, pay the bills, run errands—the list is endless! I admire women who are able to add motherhood to all these other expectations. I see the women I work with who have children, and I can only say that God must bless them with wonderful gifts of patience and time management. In the face of all these expectations, it's no wonder that we lose sight of the things that make us unique.

I've come to realize we live in an imperfect world that is constantly trying to squeeze us into the illusion of perfection. The problem is that the world's recipe for "perfection" is also the same as the recipe for a nervous breakdown. Perfection simply does not exist in this world, so you may as well give up trying to attain it and instead accept what is real. Just as we cannot live up to all of the expectations placed on us, we also cannot change who we are. God loves us just the way he made us, and Christ did not die for our sins so we could continue to be bound by worldly expectations. It's time to start living the life of joy we were given by accepting Christ as our Savior.

The first step is to see ourselves as God sees us, not as the rest of the world sees us. His is really the only opinion that matters. When I first looked at myself as I felt God saw me, I was surprised to find that my differences have not only shaped who I am, but how I serve others. I have a wonderful husband who loves me and appreciates how I am different from other people. I have a college degree because my parents made me believe that I could excel in higher education. I have a job licensing landscape architects and soil classifiers—a field that more women are entering but is still dominated by men. Most important, I am confident that with God's help I can do anything he sets before me.

—*Sherri Fulmer Moorer*

Scary Places

My husband squeezed my hand as we exited the car, walked through the musty parking garage, and entered the elevator to the medical clinic. My fate depended on the words written inside a manila folder upstairs on the fourth floor.

We sat in a small examining room, listening intently for footsteps outside the door. A giant eye glared at us from a poster on the wall as we made small talk and exchanged anxious winks and smiles. After my watch's second hand made twenty-eight unhurried rotations, footsteps paused outside, and I heard the rattle of the basket on the other side of the door as my chart was lifted. Finally the doctor walked in with stern eyes and a stiff smile. Before he spoke, I knew—but I wasn't prepared to hear the words that stripped me of all hope. "Mrs. Dawkins, I'm sorry. The lab report indicates that I removed a malignant melanoma from your eye."

Tom groaned, "No!" The color drained from his face and his knuckles turned gray. I searched my limp brain for a magic word to erase the anguish in my husband's voice and to dispel the tension in that tiny, windowless room. Yet nothing could wipe out the effect of those two overpowering words—*malignant melanoma*.

So began the adventure in which God would expose my insecurities and test my faith. He would call attention to my desperate need for his Word and my need for other people.

I knew God was not sleeping when the angry red lesion attached itself firmly at the edge of my iris. I belong to him, and he keeps me in full view at all times. I was sure he had a plan for what was happening, yet fear held me in its icy grip because I could not see what he had in mind or what he would require of me. I only knew one thing—I was inadequate!

My doctor, Dr. Mallett, was a graduate of Johns Hopkins Medical School. He was an excellent surgeon, but what I liked best about him was that he knew God. He grimaced at the sight of the monster in my eye as we discussed the possibilities at my first appointment. Yes, he could remove it, but there was the risk of impairing my sight, and worst of all there were blood vessels leading into it, indicating a threat to more than my eye. After much consideration, we reached a decision. "OK," I said, "let's schedule the surgery, and we'll pray that God will bless the work of your hands."

He responded, "Please do. I always pray before doing surgery; there's someone wiser than me up there."

So here we were, one week past surgery, and though my eye was intact and my vision normal, we sat reeling with the reality of cancer. The doctor moved closer and placed a sympathetic hand on my shoulder. "I'm not sure what we're dealing with now. There's still something there that needs to be removed. With your permission, I will send the x-rays to Johns Hopkins and get their advice before doing anything else."

Tom and I held each other up as we left the examining room, entered the elevator, and descended to the gloomy parking garage. We got in our car and drove out into the street as a light rain misted the windshield. The sunlight of that chilly February day had disappeared, and with it went our hope. The days ahead would drag on, and the battle in my mind would rage.

One day while surrounded by my family in a Chinese restaurant, I looked toward the door and saw a woman whose image would become indelibly imprinted upon my mind. The tall, elegant, dark-skinned lady was immaculately dressed in a green linen pantsuit. She wore a paisley turban on her head and a patch over her left eye. My half-eaten egg roll and sesame chicken turned cold on my plate as words from a previous phone call echoed in my memory: "Oh, my goodness! Mr. Salter had melanoma too! They took his eye out, and he endured those awful treatments that took his hair right off his head—and then he died!"

Fear, my midnight visitor, caused me to cower under the covers. I never feared dying, but I was afraid to suffer under conditions that seemed inevitable. This fear grew larger and strangled my faith. I was certain I could not measure up to the bravery I had witnessed in others who had dealt with cancer. My beautiful young friend Lynn was the most recent example. She wore her pain courageously, and her faith endured to the end. How had Lynn managed that? And, dare I even think it—why had God allowed it? I felt that God vanished the day Lynn died. These secret memories flooded my mind.

I leaned on Tom's arm as we walked into the oncology building, a place where people are transported on wheels—patients in wheelchairs and weak, pale bodies on rolling beds. I heard a child's cry and looked toward the door, where a nurse was taking a little boy from his mother's arms. I saw a young woman curled in a fetal position on a hospital gurney. She was oblivious to her surroundings, helpless and frail. I felt a strange connection to her; though my body was not confined to a hospital gurney, my spirit lay helpless, my faith paralyzed.

I was much like the paralytic in the Bible story who needed someone else's faith—someone to take hold of his stretcher, carry him up on the roof, tear a hole in it, and lower him at Jesus' feet. Similarly, I was dependent upon the strength of others, for curled within myself, bound by fear and frailty, was the fear that I could die.

As I lay in this helpless state night after night, something began to happen that I could not see or feel. When I could not pray for myself, intercessions rose to the heavens as rays of light. As the pleas entered the gates of heaven and accumulated at the throne of God, my bed—like the paralytic's mat—was moving on a secret journey, taking me closer to the feet of Jesus. As my friends and family prayed, God sent out his nudging angels to prompt people to do amazing things. One Sunday in church, Nita, my quiet friend, sat down on the pew beside me and handed me a cassette tape containing Scriptures. At night when I could not sleep, I listened to those faith-building words:

> *"Jesus touched their eyes; and instantly they received their sight…"*
> *"Great throngs accompanied Him; He healed them all…"*
> *"I Am the Lord who heals you…"*
> *"Behold, I will not forget you. I have indel-*

ibly imprinted you on the palm of each of my hands…"

Did God really have me imprinted on his hands? Would he hold me there securely, no matter what happened? Gradually the Scriptures transformed my mind, driving out the darkness of doubt and filling me with an awareness of God's presence. I began to feel his love, and I knew I could trust my future to Him.

When we finally heard from the doctor, he told us the experts at Johns Hopkins had advised him to perform a second surgery, and then a third. After the final operation, the lab report returned stating that no malignancy was present, and my oncologist reported similar findings!

In my secret thoughts, I had journeyed alone. Nevertheless, God was always there. I remembered Dr. Mallett's words: "There is someone bigger up there." That someone was the only one who knew my secret thoughts, the only one who could see the darkness shrouding my mind. When I was weak, He sent people to carry my mat and lift me out of the shadows, into the sunlight, where I could see clearly that I was at the feet of the Healer.

—*Virginia Dawkins*

Blessed with Less

Five years ago, I left the best-paying job of my career. A position with plenty of perks—travel, VIP events with the well known and well to do—it was a dream job, with opportunities to use my experience and education in foreign language. I had jumped at the opportunity—and opportunity it did present me. It was a glorious ride—for a time.

Somewhere along the way the job changed, or maybe I changed. It was a political job in the truest sense of the word, so our projects and programs depended on monies from the state legislature—ripe, rich dollars in boom times and lean, bare-bones budgets in bust times. There were more lean times than rich ones. Leadership changed frequently, and the goals became short-term and calculated to serve the leaders rather than those whom the goals were designed to serve.

What once had been my dream job became quite the opposite—a nightmare. I was miserable, and my staff was equally confused and unhappy. I shared my misery and unhappiness with anyone who would listen. My friends began to avoid my Ms. Misery persona and decline invitations to my pity parties.

One day my minister came to my office to share an idea and an invitation with me. He knew I had recently returned from an extended stay in Mexico and that I spoke and taught Spanish. For the past ten years, our church has made an annual mission trip to Bolivia to help with medical care and construction. Since they are always in need of people who are fluent in the language, my minister suggested I join the team on their upcoming trip. His description of the trip was honest, not colored by any fancy or false recruiting pitches. Instead, he told me about crossing a muddy river on a raft loaded with people, animals, and supplies; sleeping on straw mats; using outside latrines if we were lucky, but if not, just the scant privacy of the wilderness. We would be living and working with people in extreme poverty.

I was intrigued, but not convinced that this was the kind of trip I wanted to take. Although I love to travel, I am accustomed to (perhaps spoiled by) the comfort of standard amenities—indoor plumbing, hot water, a bath every day, and safe food and water. So I delayed my answer for a while, not wanting to make a hasty decision that I might regret later.

Slowly and subtly the answer came to me. A quiet, tugging inquisitiveness, much like a magnet, began pulling me inexplicably to the mystery of Bolivia. I accepted the invitation, somewhat selfishly, I admit, to escape my job for two weeks. I promised myself that I would use the time to make a decision about whether to leave my job or stay on.

The trip was everything my minister had promised, and more—hard, rough, primitive. Surprisingly, I loved it! We did indeed cross the river on a raft. We pulled our bus out of the mud when it didn't quite make it off the raft. We ate simple food, slept on straw mattresses on the floor, went to bed when the sun set, and arose when it came up the next morning. It was a mind-refreshing, soul-cleansing, and life-changing retreat from my stress-filled world.

We worked in the midst of poverty so great that I couldn't have imagined it without seeing and experiencing it. But to my amazement, just below the surface of their overwhelming needs, despite the lack and scarcity of *things*, the people had a joy and spontaneity that was missing in my life of material abundance. Although the Bolivian people don't often show happiness outwardly with smiles and laughter, I could see in them an inner peace and a faith that showed in their eyes and in their daily activities.

I wanted what these people had. Even with all my stuff, I was miserable. While they had only the clothing on their backs, simple dwellings, and just enough food, they gave me more than I could have given them. I was supposed to be the missionary, but our roles were reversed. The people I had come to help were now ministering to me in ways they didn't realize.

When I returned home, I left my job. It was an easy decision to make. Now I knew what I wanted. A fancy job with all the perks and the accompanying stress no longer fit my needs or my dreams. Giving up a regular salary, perks, parties, and comfortable, exotic travel for financial insecurity and no definite job sure made some of my friends and family question my sanity and of course the direction of my career path, which seemed to be moving downward.

Now that I am self-employed, I do have less materially and financially, but I have more spiritually. My needs are simpler and are more than adequately met. My dreams and goals have changed to be more spiritual than material. I am much happier, and everyone around me is too. It's more fun to share happiness than misery, and your friends don't try to avoid you!

Within the word *blessing* is the small word *less*. In a far-off, unfamiliar land, high in the Andes Mountains, away from the rush and stress of our consumer-oriented culture, I learned that sometimes you have to give things up in your life and live with less to experience the abundance of God's blessings. Amid the material poverty of Bolivia, I found spiritual wealth and the simple abundance of God's love and blessings. I now have abundance in the part of my life where I needed it most.

My minister often reminds us that we are blessed so we can be a blessing. I went to Bolivia to be a blessing and to serve, yet the irony and mystery of my experience is that I received greater blessings than I gave.

Each year, about three months before the annual mission trip, I begin to feel the gentle tugs and hear the faint whispers calling me back to Bolivia. Like a vague homesickness, Bolivia calls me back to what is real and what is true in life, the simple abundance of God's love and blessings. Blessed with less materially, but much more spiritually, I return to Bolivia every year for a refresher course—my spiritual sabbatical on what is really important in life.

—*Linda E. Allen*

A Whisper in the Lilacs

"It's May. The lilacs are in bloom," I thought. Lilacs are my favorite flower. I love their rich purple hue and strong perfumelike scent. Their fragrance fills the whole house, and their presence in any room announces that spring has arrived. This particular spring, however, I could not enjoy them, nor did I think I would make it home to see them before their brief blooming period was over. My life at the moment revolved around a hospital room on the pediatric floor of Mt. Sinai Hospital. The sight of spring flowers in bloom had been replaced by intravenous tubes and heart monitors. The inescapable odor of alcohol swabs and latex gloves overpowered any memory of fragrant blossoms.

It seemed strange to be thinking about lilacs at a time like that. At seven weeks old, our first child, Ryan, had just been diagnosed with a rare, life-threatening liver disease called biliary atresia. He had survived a demanding, six-hour surgery to build a new bile duct from his intestines and to remove his nonfunctioning gallbladder. The previous seven weeks had been a nightmare of sleepless nights, doctor visits, diagnostic tests, and fear, all culminating in this life-saving surgery.

While my husband and I were still in shock after the surgery, trying to recover from the trauma of handing our baby over to surgeons, nurses, and anesthesiologists, we were given a discouraging prognosis that, naively, we had not anticipated. We expected to hear that all was well and that our son was on the road to recovery and a normal life. Instead, the doctors were telling us Ryan was not out of danger—in fact, he never would be. Their words seemed to be meant for someone else as I heard them say things like "incurable," "chronic," "serious," "complications." They told us that the surgery had saved Ryan's life and might have bought him some time, but they gently explained he would always be a sick boy, suffering from infections and possibly requiring a restricted diet. Chances were good that he would eventually need a liver transplant.

Maybe it was too much to absorb all at once; or perhaps it's the soul's way of survival in time of crisis; or maybe I was able, on some subconscious level, to trust God for a miracle; but I remember thinking to myself, "Everything will seem so much brighter if I can get home and see my lilacs blooming."

Looking back, I see it was the simple gestures of those who showed their concern in ways that came naturally for them that left a lasting impression. A card from a teacher colleague read, "My mother's heart breaks for yours." Those words are forever etched in my mind. Sally, one of the nurses, faithfully made Ryan's crib each morning she was on duty because she knew I liked his little bed to be neat. My sister-in-law brought us simple takeout meals, and my mother-in-law slipped twenty-dollar bills to my husband to help us pay for gas and parking.

Then there was the vase of purple lilacs from the mother of one of my first-grade students. She didn't know lilacs were my favorite flower. She hadn't heard my thoughts of longing to be home to see them in bloom. She couldn't have known, but God did. What she did know was the pain of a mother's heart when her child is sick. She understood the fear of being told your newborn baby is not healthy. She could relate to the anguish, the uncertainty, the aloneness, and the shock of life suddenly taking a turn down an unexpected and irreversible road. Her son had been born with a severe disability, so she had walked down this path. She was still traveling that road, dodging potholes and unmarked curves.

Kind as she was, she didn't try to give me useless advice, make empty promises, or spout spiritual platitudes. She simply brought me a vase of lavender lilacs and a smile. Through her actions, she spoke to me of God's love and faithfulness. She showed me empathy, not merely sympathy, and she communicated hope—that life continues and that I would find joy in simple pleasures again. The sight of those lilacs assured me I would adjust to this challenge, and I could count on God to be with me. This fellow mom acted on her heart's impulse, and through the simple gesture of clipping some lilacs from her garden, God used her to remind me that he had not forgotten me. Not only was he still in control, but he also heard the unspoken desires of my heart.

God's faithful love sustained me through many months of pain and worry, and for reasons I will never understand fully, He granted our family a modern-day miracle. Ryan now shows no signs of liver disease and leads the normal, raucous life of the average ten-year-old. The doctors' worst predictions never came to be, and I have never again missed a season of lilacs. God proved to me that his grace is indeed sufficient and that no matter what I may face in this life, he has promised never to leave me nor forsake me.

God reminded me of his promises in much the same way he spoke to Elijah, the Old Testament prophet, when he became discouraged and fearful. Elijah looked for God to speak to him in an earthquake, a strong wind, and a fire, but instead God showed up in what the Bible calls "a gentle whisper."

In much the same way, God did not use the ability of doctors, the whirlwind of sympathetic visitors, or the most advanced medical technology to reassure me of his unwavering faithfulness. Instead he used another mother and the flowers I longed to see. Through them he whispered to my heart, "See, I have not forgotten you."

—Mary Gallagher

Cathedral Building

I stood on the stone sidewalk and tilted my head back as far as I could. I could barely see the tops of the two great towers of Notre Dame. I could hardly believe I was there! For two years I'd planned to take the trip of my lifetime to England and France. I'd been through a painful divorce and a humiliating bankruptcy, then a grueling midlife career change. My divorce lawyer had been upset with me when I settled for the fifty-year-old, rundown house instead of taking the savings and mutual funds, but I didn't want my daughters to lose their home as well as their father's daily presence. Three years later—with new plumbing, a new roof, and a paint job—I sold the house and was able to buy a larger but less expensive place where the girls could have their own rooms. And the extra profit from the house would pay for a trip to Paris for my younger daughter, Martine, and me—praise God!

Notre Dame was our first stop on our first day. The tour began outside the magnificent facade, where we marveled at the soaring towers and intricate statuary. All the figures, large and small, have meaning and significance. They represent human knowledge, virtues, and vices. The center door of the cathedral portrays the Last Judgment, where the saints gather thankfully to Jesus' right side and the condemned are taken away in chains to his left. Even the very lines of the building have meaning. Cardinal Feltin (archbishop of Paris from 1949 to 1966) said of Notre Dame, "The upward yearning of its arches and its spires expresses the movement of prayer in which the soul lifts itself to God who is Spirit and Love."

Built in the then newfangled Gothic style, Notre Dame's pillars and buttresses made it possible to have more windows for a lighter interior. And, oh, what windows they are! Two glorious rose windows, one to the north and one to the south, fascinate the eye like a child's kaleidoscope. Thirteen meters in diameter, the huge windows contain scenes from the Scriptures—Old Testament in the north window, New Testament in the south—but Jesus is at the center of both, being the prophecy of one and the fulfillment of the other. The colors blaze in the sunlight, royal purples and blues and reds.

As I stood awestruck beside the fence in front of the cathedral, I spied a tiny spider's web on the fence itself. A thought came to me that I believe was actually whispered by a still, small voice: The great building before me is a cathedral, but the spider's web is, too!

It took human architects and artists 200 years to complete Notre Dame, with a succession of kings patronizing their work. It takes a solitary spider only a night to complete a web, but it is no less a marvel of engineering. The spider's cathedral is supported by strands of silk rather than flying buttresses, yet by weight, that silk is stronger than steel rope. Notre Dame is built in the Gothic style, a term that was applied pejoratively at first, meaning "barbaric." However, spiders construct webs of as many styles as there are architectural schools. Some cast their webs like fishermen cast nets; others throw sticky-ended strings of web like Argentinean vaqueros throw bolas. Spiders can build webs that resemble funnels, sheets, spirals, or wheels. Each one is a marvel of engineering, with the blueprints carried in the spider's genes!

While the cathedral has carvings depicting the four seasons, the stages of life, and daily work, the spider's web *is* daily work, carried out through the seasons and stages of life. The spider has to maintain his web and repair it often, yet people also have to repair Notre Dame. During the French Revolution, the church was damaged by people rejecting faith for reason, authority for anarchy. The cathedral was put up for sale and could have been quarried for its stones. But faith returned, and the cathedral was restored. Again it was threatened as bombs fell in Europe during the World Wars. Even today, it requires constant care. In fact, while I was there, scaffolding covered the side of one tower and the apse. After all, Notre Dame is an elderly lady; she celebrated her first Mass in 1185. But that span of time is the blink of an eye compared to the millennia that spiders have been building their edifices, a millisecond compared to our eternal Creator!

For while men and spiders are each great architects in their ways, the greatest architect of all is God. He has designed our universe to spin more magnificently than the finest Swiss watch works. The biosystem of the Earth (without human interference) functions more perfectly than the best-designed zoo exhibit. Each creature in God's creation is a testament to his wisdom and power. Each web, nest, lair, dam, and burrow is a cathedral for the Creator who gave that being life. Should our efforts be any less?

It seems so obvious to me now that the structures we build with our hands to glorify God are no greater or lesser accomplishments than the delicate web of the spider. I've also learned that not all cathedrals are made of stone, wood, hay, or even silk. Our cathedrals are built with days. Each day of our lives is a stone in the edifice of our praise. When we live badly, we tear down our cathedral, as I did during my dark days of failure. But by God's grace, we can rebuild, restore, purify, and maintain our temples. "Or do you not know that your body is the temple of the Holy Spirit who is in you, whom you have from God, and you are not your own?" (1 Corinthians 6:19, NKJV). A life well lived according to God's law and by his grace is a well-built tribute to his glory. I've already begun my "renovation," but there's much more to do.

—Devon France

Speaking of Faith . . .

Korlane, one of the college students in my public speaking class, walked up to me before class and whimpered, "Can't you just choose a topic for me, Mr. Drum? It doesn't really matter what my topic is, does it? This is just speech class. Nobody really listens to other people speak." Korlane certainly did know how to make me feel good about my teaching discipline. Still, if I had a penny for every time a student had said this to me the weekend before speeches were due, I would be a mogul of the copper-tubing industry. It is a disturbing trend—so many young people have so little faith that they can make a difference to anyone else. It is a symptom of a world that has slowly convinced generations of people that life matters only when a person achieves great things in significant ways. But we couldn't be more wrong.

I looked at this young lady, seeing the potential she couldn't. I asked her to think about experiences in her life that were emotionally moving, persuasive, angering, frustrating, or simply interesting.

"Like what?" she asked, peeking over the top of her glasses like a wise old granny.

"I don't know. Everyone has something different to share. Your view of life is unique, and it's quite possible that something you have experienced or observed is a subject someone else needs to hear about. Perhaps somebody in your family works for a company you admire. You could talk about that company or the careers it offers. Or, on a more serious note, maybe you have a friend who has suffered through a tragedy, and you want to inform others about how to be helpful to friends in need. Who knows? Maybe you're a pizza connoisseur, and you can tell us all how to make the perfect pizza right in our own homes. See what I'm getting at, Korlane?"

She nodded at me, the gears starting to spin. "Thanks for the help. I'll see you Monday." I quickly reminded her to call or e-mail if she needed any more help over the weekend. I had a gut feeling I might hear from her, but Saturday and Sunday ticked by with no communication. I took that as a good sign.

Monday morning arrived and lugged with it sleepy students dressed in casually formal, albeit wrinkled, attire. You could tell it was a speech day and that most students were ill equipped to work the complexities of an iron before 8:00 A.M. I arrived in the classroom a few minutes early to check out the audio-visual equipment, and I noticed Korlane in the back, rehearsing quietly. "Looks like you figured something out," I said with a bit of reassurance in my voice.

"Can I go last? I need to work up my nerve before I speak." She paused for a moment but started up again before I could answer. "I don't know if my speech will knock anyone's socks off, but I feel good about the topic I've chosen. You really helped me figure it all out on Friday, Mr. Drum."

"Last you are, Korlane. Consider it your reward for all of your hard work. I'll look forward to hearing what you have to say." I smiled, proud that she had found her voice. As other students began pouring into the class in their mummylike states, Korlane took her seat and continued to go over her note cards. I made a few announcements and reminded the class about the timing signals that I would use in order to help them properly pace themselves in their speeches.

I moved to my seat and called for the first speaker. I listened to speeches on topics ranging from how to properly sheer the hair off a sheep to how to quickly create irresistible pickup lines to fanatical arguments about why golf should not be considered a real sport. It was a tasty smorgasbord of topics that kept class lively and interesting.

Finally the time came for Korlane to give her speech. She smiled nervously as she stood and made her way to the podium. Her first words were sturdy, full of confidence, and quickly tuned the audience in to the personal nature of her speech. "A few months ago, I was diagnosed with depression. For a long time, I had felt helpless about life and came to a point where I cried every day and often wished I could find a way to end my life quickly. A lot of people suffer quietly from depression. Today I want to help you to be able to identify the signs of depression and give you ideas about helping such people with their pain and struggles."

Korlane's willingness to share such a personal side of her life captivated the audience, and when she finished, a few class members stood up to hug her while others wiped tears from their eyes. One student in particular sat motionless, immersed in her private thoughts, large tears trickling down her cheeks.

Korlane came over to me and quietly asked, "Did I say something wrong that made her cry?"

"No, you didn't say anything wrong, Korlane." I patted her on the back. "Your speech may have just reminded her of some tough memories or something. Don't worry; I'll take care of it. You did a very good job. I'm proud of you."

"Thanks." She grabbed her backpack and began to walk out of class, glancing back at the other student, worry in her eyes.

I made my way over to the tearful and distressed young woman. I knelt down in front of her and said I would listen if she needed to talk. She looked at me with bloodshot, glassy eyes and began telling me a story that left me speechless. "I came to class today," her voice filled with a rush of emotion, "only to tell you good-bye."

I spoke softly. "Are you going somewhere? Has something happened?"

"No, Mr. D., I came here to say good-bye for good. I wrote you this note." She took it from her bag and slid it across the desk to me. She then reached back into the bag and started to speak again. "I was also going to swallow these pills in the bathroom after class," she whispered as she handed me a bottle, weeping a river of tears. "I thought I was alone with all of these feelings of despair that were tearing up my heart. I thought it was just me, alone with this craziness in my mind." She paused to calm her tears, but to no avail. "I don't want to die. I want to feel better."

I reached out to hold her hand, and she rested her head on my arm and let her pain pour out in deep sobs, gushing tears, and what seemed to be sighs of relief releasing the secret that was killing her.

Two days later, Korlane showed up at my office looking a little down. "What's up?" I asked.

"Oh, I feel stupid. Since my speech the other day a few people have started to sort of treat me different, like something is wrong with me. On top of that, I just cannot stop thinking about that girl who was crying after class. What kind of speech makes someone cry like that? I probably should have talked about how to bake cookies or something."

"Hmm." I leaned toward her to make sure I got her attention. "I have something I was told to give to you. I think it might make you feel better." I pulled an envelope from my desk, handed it to her, and leaned back in my chair. "Read this before you say anything else."

Korlane looked at me with wide eyes. She slowly opened the letter and unfolded it with care. As her eyes moved over each line of the letter, I could see overwhelming emotions rush through her cheeks and tears begin to well in her eyes. She whispered the question rolling through her mind. "I did this?"

"Yes. You helped to save this girl's life. She wanted to say thank you to you but didn't know how before she left for home. So I encouraged her to write you a note and tell you how she felt. This is what she wrote." I pointed to the letter in her hands.

"She said she wants me to call her so we can talk." Korlane said. "What do I say to her?"

"Say what comes from your heart, Korlane. Your willingness to share the story about your depression gave her hope. She didn't feel alone anymore. Speak from your heart, and I'm sure whatever you say will be just fine."

"I guess I could do that," she said with a bit of both timidity and hope in her voice.

"Remember when I told the class that even your smallest words can have great power? We may not think what we are saying makes a difference, but we can never know that. That's why we need to measure all our words with care, especially since we now realize that seeds of hope can be planted even in a speech class." Korlane smiled at me, held the letter to her chest, and told me she needed to make a phone call. In that moment, my heart was full to overflowing, uplifted with a new sense of faith, hope, and love.

This event reaffirmed my belief that all of our actions and words, whether small or large in scope, are sacred, potent, and chock-full of potential. Indeed, if faith is what we hope for, then the unexpected gift of hope shared that day in my classroom was nothing less than a testament to the miraculous and mysterious power of God at work. I am humbly reminded that even my small and unwitting encouragement of a college student who was apprehensive about speaking could be a part of God's healing hand.

Korlane's message is God's enduring proclamation to us all: We are never alone.

—*Matthew Nelson Drumheller*

Healed from the Inside Out

The year I learned my biggest lesson in Sunday school, I was in the girls' fourth grade class at the Baptist church where I grew up. We were all around ten years old, the age when children begin to form cliques that contain a few choice friends and exclude others who might not fit for whatever reason. Though I sang in the choir and participated in children's memory class, I wasn't destined to become a member of the "in" crowd. My father, a pipe fitter, was seasonally unemployed, and my mother struggled to make ends meet with a part-time office position. In the 1960s, it seemed to me that many families were financially secure if not affluent, but my family struggled to make ends meet. When the church brought us a basket of food one Thanksgiving, I was both grateful and embarrassed. Thankfully, none of the girls in Sunday school knew of the gift, but in the back of my mind I worried they would find out.

Each Sunday morning I sat with one girl or another. In our group of fifteen, only ten or twelve came routinely. Of these, six formed a tight "in" group with two or three "satellites," who were only "in," if the other girls deemed them acceptable on a given Sunday. Sometimes I was one of those satellites, at other times a wandering star sitting on the fringes of the small universe that was our little class.

Annette Culver, one of the unfavored few, seemed a little brighter than the other outsiders. I was drawn to her intelligent and sensitive expression, even though her body was badly misshapen by polio, her legs bound by braces, her small figure supported by crutches. I had known her for so many years at our church that I did not give her appearance much thought. But that year I became aware of her spirit. She always seemed to know the right answers to the teacher's questions. I appreciated her sitting with me on the days when I was an outsider, but I failed to think of her on those rare Sundays when the clique allowed me to join them.

That year at Easter my mother finally gave in to my annual plea for a new Easter dress. I had heard the other girls talking excitedly about the styles and colors they had chosen, and I did not want to be left out again as I so often was, for instance, when they talked of their family's new cars or summer vacations.

Mom was kind but firm. "We'll go to Goodwill. That's all we can afford this year, honey."

Crestfallen, I agreed. Even a used dress was better than none at all.

Browsing racks of donated clothing, I finally settled on a dress made of white chiffon-type fabric with thin, black thread shot through it in a zigzag pattern, and transparent short sleeves. While it was not what I would have chosen at a department store, it was "new" for me and would have to do.

On Easter Sunday I combed my long, dark hair, securing each side with a plastic barrette. Slipping into my new finery, I felt almost pretty. In Sunday school I took my place beside Annette, demurely looking around to see if anyone would notice. I saw that Annette wore a dark jumper and short-sleeved white blouse, one of her usual outfits. Her thick blonde curls were pushed back with a headband.

"You look nice," I offered politely, still hoping the other girls would say something about my new dress.

"So do you," she replied. "Say, that's a pretty dress. Did you get it for Easter?"

Finally I had gotten the praise I was after, even if it was only from Annette. "Yes!" I murmured excitedly. "And it cost only eighty-nine cents at Goodwill!"

I rewarded my faithful companion with honesty. But I had not counted on the fact that Joanie Jameson, the class gossip, could hear from her seat behind us.

Snorting, she loudly repeated my news as the other girls in their pretty pastel dresses with matching purses and white gloves turned to hear. "Eighty-nine cents! Your mom bought that at Goodwill?"

Several girls laughed as my face burned. Thankfully, Mrs. Brown arrived then and began taking attendance. Annette reached over and touched my hand. "It's beautiful," she said, sincerity shining in her eyes.

Annette's kindness that day cemented our friendship. When Joanie or Carla or one of the other girls beckoned me to a vacant seat among "the group" on later Sundays, I looked to see if there was a second seat for Annette.

"Thanks, but I already have one," I replied to such an invitation one late spring morning as I sat beside Annette. I asked her if her limbs hurt, noticing for the first time the uncomfortable fold of her knees in their metal clasps. She smiled and said no. As spring marched into summer, Annette began missing Sundays. The next time she came, I noticed she had a slight wheeze.

"Are you okay?" I asked anxiously.

She nodded, a little out of breath. "My parents want me to see this specialist," she explained.

Immediately I became anxious. On such a tight budget, my family seldom saw specialists except for serious illnesses, like when my dad got pneumonia after working outdoors on winter construction.

"I'll pray for you," I said, and Annette smiled appreciatively.

Annette did not return for several weeks. When she did, I was shocked by her appearance. Moving slowly on her crutches and braces, her face was pale, eyes tired. Sitting beside her in Sunday school, I was afraid to ask how she was doing, but I sat a little closer, as though to protect her.

Sensing my anxiety, Annette looked up, for she was somewhat bent over, and smiled feebly. "Don't worry about me. I'm having an operation on Tuesday."

"Are you afraid?" I asked, petrified at the thought.

"No," she said steadily, "because if they don't fix me, I'll be with Jesus, and I know he will."

Tears tightened my throat, preventing a reply. Silently I prayed, "Lord, please fix Annette. She's so good."

The other girls were oblivious. There was a look of concern on Mrs. Brown's face during prayer time as she listed requests on the blackboard. She mentioned Annette as I started to raise my hand.

"Annette is having surgery this week. It'll take several hours. Let's pray for the Lord to guide her doctor's hands and for a safe and speedy recovery."

The next few days I worried, my friend haunting my thoughts. On Tuesday I asked my mom if we could pray together. After that, a peace came over me. I would leave it up to God.

The following Sunday morning, I arrived at class early and took a post at the door, waiting for the others to arrive. While I didn't expect Annette to come the first Sunday following her grueling surgery, I needed to feel connected to God and to her. At first there was just a trickle of children in the hall finding their classrooms and sharing greetings and good-humored comments. Then, as the trickle grew into a steady stream, I saw a mass of blonde curls in the sea of heads coming down the hall toward me. My heart began to race. It couldn't be! Staring and staring until the sea parted, I glimpsed the bright features I knew so well. A moment later her gaze met mine, eyes brightening. Yet she wasn't close enough to hear me. Another minute or so and she would be here. I couldn't get over her face—so clear of pain, with a healthy color. She even appeared to be walking straighter and without the aid of her crutches. Had the doctors completely cured her?

The crowd of boys and girls closed her off from my view once more, until seconds later she had almost reached the door of our classroom. Catching another glimpse of her face turned my way, I called, "Annette! You're healed!"

She nodded happily, though she did not speak. As the crowd of kids began to thin in the hallway, some going this way, others that, I saw my dear friend walking easily, without crutches for the first time—I was elated!

But Annette kept going, not stopping to enter our classroom. Several steps beyond our door, still flanked by children heading to their classes, she turned and waved. Puzzled, I went into our classroom and sat down. Maybe she was getting a drink from the water fountain. Or perhaps she was going to talk to a former teacher. I waited and waited, but she did not return.

Although I was disappointed Annette had passed me by, I was so eager to share the joy of her recovery with the rest of the class, I scarcely noticed the girls filling our classroom. Christie, a red-haired girl of eleven, asked if the seat beside me was taken. "No," I offered, "would you like to sit with me?" I saved the seat on my other side for Annette in case she came back. I reflected with some amazement that I was becoming more sociable with other girls in Annette's absence. No longer did I feel like an outsider, nor did I want other girls in our class to feel left out. Mrs. Brown took her place solemnly before us. As she began to speak, I roused myself to catch her opening words.

"I'm sorry to tell you that Annette passed away this week, following her surgery. Her funeral was yesterday."

Raising my hand, I interjected excitedly, "But I just saw her—she's fine! She's here!"

With a sad look, Mrs. Brown shook her head. "I'm sorry, Debbie. It must have been someone who looks like her. Annette's in heaven now."

Overcome by this revelation, I thought it over as Mrs. Brown began to teach our Bible lesson. It had to have been someone that looked like my friend, but it was enough to remind me that she had been right. Though the doctors couldn't fix her, she had gone on to someone who did. I was touched that she had taken a moment to share her recovery with me in the place that had fused our friendship and directed our faith. I knew she would not return to see me again, but someday I will go to her. Thanks to her quiet example, I have made it a point to look for the "left out" girls and women in social settings and to invite them to sit with me. God healed both Annette *and* me—from the inside out.

—*Debra Johanyak*

Disturbing the Waters

"How could they do this to me?"

I kicked a pebble off the path I was walking on and shook my head. I might expect to be gossiped about at work, but to experience such a blatant display of tongue-wagging at church was something I thought couldn't happen. That people who claimed to follow in Jesus' footsteps believed lies about me was even more shocking. All they had to do was ask me, instead of relying on the chain of church communication, which, while it kept things in order, also had the potential to cause misunderstandings when taken for granted.

I was hurt and angry. I felt so betrayed that I felt I didn't even know the people I'd spent the past ten years serving with. If they could so easily believe what another woman said about me without even checking the facts, how could I call them my "brethren"?

The actions of my fellow Christians proved to me that they were far from perfect. But the experience I'd had that afternoon seemed so brazen, so un-Christian that I didn't know what to think. At a meeting earlier that day, another woman claimed that the work and ideas I'd poured into children's church were her own, and she also claimed that I hadn't done my share of the work.

So I did what I usually did to hash things out. I walked. As I walked, I prayed. People could be blind, but God knew what was right. "Lord, if you see everything, why did you allow her to take over like that? Why did you let her lie about me? Why did you allow others to believe the lies she told about me?"

I didn't expect an answer. I was so miserable that I didn't pay attention to where I was going. The path meandered through a mixed woodland and wetland area, so I did too. I followed a squirrel as it searched for acorns, climbed partway up a branching evergreen, and discovered a hidden bird's nest. Gradually, my movements formed a pattern. Though I'd thought my walking was aimless, my steps led me to one of the places I often went to seek God's presence. I'd felt so frustrated that I hadn't planned to visit this special place, but apparently there was a greater reason for my choice of direction than I was conscious of.

I rounded a clump of ferns and arrived at a small pond. Beside the pool grew a immense weeping willow with a huge, crinkled trunk that felt good to lean against. Its drooping fronds caressed the right side of the pond, making a cool spot for fish to con-gregate on hot afternoons. I sat beneath the tree and skipped a few stones. The tiny pebbles spread rings of ripples where they touched the surface of the water.

I frowned, thinking, "See how easy it is to dis-turb peaceful waters?" But the waters didn't look disturbed. As soon as the ripples reached the water's edge, the surface returned to its untroubled state.

Still frowning, I skipped another rock. The reflected reds and golds of the evening sky danced across the ripples before once again becoming still and clear. Interesting. When the reflections were disturbed, they didn't shrink back, as I had after the committee meeting. They danced. Then they regained their composure on the calm surface. Was it the stillness of the water that made the pond so peaceful, or was it actually waiting for a disturbance, like a skipping stone, to make it dance?

I skipped another rock. As the reflections of the sky and trees wavered in the pool, I realized that the pond mirrored a world that reached far beyond its own boundaries. The waters could be still, or they could dance. As I skipped another rock, I was smiling. I had my answer—one I wasn't expecting. I'd thought that Christianity had failed that day in the meeting, when the waters of my expectations had been disturbed. I'd had the idea that because I shared a dedication to Jesus with my Christian brothers and sisters, I wouldn't have to face misunderstanding. I'd assumed that working with Christians meant I'd never have to stand up for what was right. That was something I might have to do outside the church, but I'd believed that within church walls I was safe from human error.

The waters of the pool reminded me that other Christians, and even I myself, are human. God's overreaching purpose was bigger than my troubles or human weaknesses. I had been compartmentalizing Christian behavior into what was supposed to happen at church and what could happen outside of church. That had put me into a state of denial, so I believed that if I didn't *see* any faults in my Christian brothers and sisters, those faults didn't exist. The faith of the members of my church group may have faltered when they misjudged me, but so had mine.

The ideas Jesus taught are bigger than any committee meeting or my own feelings of betrayal. I realized that I needed to be ready to stand up, not for myself, but for the principles of honesty, kindness, and love that Jesus came to earth to teach. Instead of shutting down when I saw faith falter, that's where God's work in me needed to begin. Instead of seeing a painful experience as a betrayal, I needed to see it as an opportunity for my faith to grow. Giving in to gossip didn't mean that my Christian brothers and sisters had lost their faith or that God hadn't seen what happened. He'd just given me an opportunity to show what my relationship with Him was really made of.

Now I could return to church not only with renewed hope but with a stronger resolve to live as I believed. I smiled with relief when I realized I didn't need the anger or hurt I'd felt to set things right. All I needed was to remember what Jesus taught—it's not by our perfection that people will recognize who follows in his steps; it's by how well we love one another. After seeing the calm surface of the pond dance in response to the disturbance of my skipping stones, I came to believe that love is a whole lot more resilient than I'd thought.

—*Kriss Erickson*

Though He Stumble . . .

The group of tourists was out for a game walk along Zimbabwe's magnificent Zambezi River. Despite the hot sunshine, dust, swarms of midges, and various other discomforts, they were enjoying themselves. The searing October heat, which precedes the summer rains, has its advantages. One of these is that it is easier to spot wild game. The dry bushveld and lack of surface water help to bring the creatures out into the open, making them easier to see. Unfortunately, it can also make them skittish and bad tempered.

This particular group of tourists had come across an exceptional sight: a group of wild painted dogs were feasting on a recent kill. The predators, so named because of the random splotches of vivid color on their coats, are very rare and therefore well worth the video footage the group accorded them.

The safari guide, Dave Christensen, was standing a few feet behind the tourists, talking to them and answering their questions; all spoke in very low voices. Ever vigilant for dangerous wildlife, Dave kept his weapon loaded and a wary eye out over the rest of the bushveld. He was keeping particular tabs on a small group of elephants not far behind them.

Without warning, one female elephant suddenly took umbrage and began charging toward the group with deadly intent. "Hey!" shouted Dave, trying to deflect her course. But she continued undeterred. Dave turned to face her, lifting the heavy weapon at the same time. As he did so, he tripped over a stump, leaving him no time to line up a clear shot. The elephant was almost on top of him. He was forced to fire from the hip in a kneeling position. But Dave's aim was true. The bullet found its mark, killing the elephant instantly. But her weight gave her enough forward momentum that she sent Dave flying before she finally came to a halt in the dust, her trunk flung out on top of the same stump over which Dave had just tripped.

The loud report from Dave's gun startled everything else in the nearby vicinity. Clouds of birds nobody had even realized were present erupted from the trees into the air, chattering with fright. The tourists scattered. The person holding the video camera did not stop filming, and for a few seconds, the footage went wild.

It took a good few minutes to calm everyone down and take stock of the situation in which they had so suddenly found themselves. One second they were enjoying peaceful scenes of wildlife, the next their lives were in danger.

Although the video had been recording the painted dogs, the microphone picked up Dave's shout—and just 3.8 seconds later, the gunshot. That was all the difference between life and death for Dave, who was placed between the angry elephant and his clients. Just 3.8 seconds. What had made the difference?

That same day, I was at home alone several hundred kilometers away in Zimbabwe's capital city, Harare. It had been a quiet day and, I had taken advantage of a rare moment of solitude to brew up a pot of tea and study my Bible. But for some reason, concentration was impossible. I kept thinking about my young friend, Dave Christensen. Somehow the Lord communicated to me an urgency to pray for him. So I set aside everything else and began to pray. Since I did not know exactly what to pray for, I asked the Lord to help me with a verse from Scripture. The words, "Read Psalm 37:23-24" sprang to mind. I opened my Bible and read:

> *If the Lord delights in a man's way,*
> *He makes his steps firm:*
> *Though he stumble he will not fall,*

For the Lord upholds him with his hand.

I prayed until the need to pray finally seeped away, and my task as an intercessor was complete. If anything significant had happened, I would find out in due course.

The next evening I went to church as usual to attend our regular youth service. Afterward Dave's mother came up to chat with me.

"We could have lost Dave yesterday," she began. I went cold as she told me what had transpired the day before, how he had in fact tripped over a stump and that it could have cost him his life.

"Now let me share with you what happened to me yesterday," I told her when she had finished. "I had no idea anything was wrong with Dave, but I was praying for him. Probably the exact words God used to pull him through."

Together we read the verse from Psalms.

"Although he stumbled, he did not fall. If he had fallen, the elephant would have killed him," she said. "Do you think God was using his Word to protect Dave?"

"I believe so," I replied.

"It was really close," she said. We were both a bit shaky.

I decided to talk to our minister about it. "We talk about prayers of intercession, but does God really need them? Why does he use them? He is all-powerful—can he not work on his own, without those prayers?" I asked. "What if I had not prayed for Dave yesterday? Would it have made any difference?"

"The Scriptures talk about people standing in the gap and making up a hedge of protection. God does the rest," was his reply to my question.

Certainly, I cannot claim any glory. All I did was speak a few words, hundreds of kilometers away from the action. I did not even know what had happened. It was God who did the important part.

A few weeks later, I went with a group to visit the Christensen home. Since the Christensens farmed some distance from Harare, we made it a day trip. There they showed us photographs of the elephant, and we watched the video as well.

"Do you know I've come to realize that God is not a God who is far away? He really is that close by," said someone. For the most part, we were silent, thinking about the various implications of God's love for individuals and of intercessory prayer.

It was a life-changing experience for those involved. It brought all of us closer together. Dave and his family, who would never again take prayers for his safety for granted, realized that beyond any shadow of a doubt the Lord's hand was upon him when he needed it most.

For me, it was a truly overwhelming experience to be such a vital, alive part of God's kingdom. I felt he allowed me that experience because he is gracious. He could have done it on his own, yet instead he chose to work through me. Is this not great evidence of his love for me? It was only the first time the Lord worked through my prayers in such a way, yet every time a prayer is answered, it is so splendidly fulfilling! I keep thinking, "Wow! This is the God of the whole universe, yet he is so concerned about each and every one of us in such a personal way."

—*Mrs. C. A. Tucker*

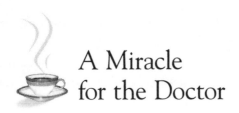

A Miracle
for the Doctor

Fran Rogers was lying in the operating room of the hospital, prepared for the removal of a malignant tumor in her left breast. The surgeon was late. She lay there waiting, gazing up at the skylight above.

"Lord," she said, "if any healing takes place, you are going to have to do it anyway. The doctor who is scheduled to do this operation doesn't know you or your healing power. If you would heal me right now, it would be a wonderful way for him to see that there is a Physician greater than he!"

She felt perfect peace descend on her. Immediately she knew she was healed.

A few minutes later the doctor came in. "Do you want chloroform or ether?" he asked.

"Neither," she answered.

"Well, I can't do this operation without an anesthetic," he said.

"You don't have to do it," she told him. "While you were gone, another doctor came and did it for you."

"What doctor?" he asked.

"Well, I don't think you know him," she answered. "It was the Great Physician!"

She said no more, for she wanted to provoke his curiosity.

When the doctor saw that Fran was convinced that she had been healed, he called in several other doctors, one of whom was a Christian, and explained the situation to them.

"Well, let's look at her x-rays again," said one.

"You needn't look at them," Fran said. "They don't apply any more."

But for their own sake, they took her down for some more x-rays.

The doctors stared at the new x-rays in surprise. The Christian doctor exclaimed, "She's right! The lump is gone!" The other doctors looked somewhat uncomfortable. But they released Fran from the hospital that day, and she went home.

That night Fran's phone rang. It was her surgeon. "I wonder if you would mind," he said, "if my wife and I came out to your home and talked to you."

"I'd be happy for you to come,"

While Fran awaited their visit, she sat down with her Bible and made a list of Scripture verses she wanted her doctor to read. When he and his wife arrived, he exclaimed, "I want to hear what really happened to you!"

"You really want to know why the operation wasn't necessary?"

"Yes, I really do."

"Well, you were late," she answered. "And as I lay there looking up at the skylight in the operating room, I prayed and asked the Lord to heal me. God answered that prayer."

"Did any minister come in and lays hands on you?"

"No, sir. This was just a prayer straight up. It was just a prayer that it could be done—and that it might be done—and it was."

The doctor stared at Fran in amazement. "You have no fear of it coming back?" he asked.

"No, sir, the Lord healed it," she replied. "Many physicians do not realize that Jesus had a healing ministry as well as a teaching and preaching one. I believe he has just as much power to heal today as he did when he was on this earth. But I want you to know, too, Doctor, that if Jesus had wanted me to endure that operation, or even death, I would have been content to do so! For I submit to his will, and I realize that it's not always his will to heal. In this case, I believe he did it that he might be glorified."

Then Fran told the doctor and his wife about how Jesus Christ had died for their sins, arose from the grave, and lives today. "You see the evidence that he lives today," she said, "in what he has done for me!"

Several weeks later the surgeon called Fran again. "I've read all the Bible verses you gave me," he said. "I would like you to make me another list with verses on how one becomes a Christian."

"I'll be glad to," Fran answered. "I'll have it ready when you come."

When the doctor came to Fran's home a second time, she gave him the list. "The first verse on this list is, 'Believe on the Lord Jesus Christ, and thou shalt be saved,'" she said. "If you and your wife will do that, you will be saved—you'll be born into God's family—you'll be Christians."

"Well, we will certainly look up these verses and give them a lot of thought," he answered. "We already got a lot out of that first list you made up, and we appreciate your going to this trouble."

"It's no trouble," Fran assured him. "Tell me, do you go to church anywhere?"

"No."

"I wish you would start going," she said, "because you need to learn more of God's Word. The life of every person you operate on is in your hands. As a Christian, you would realize your dependence on God and seek his guidance before every operation."

"Well, we'll think about it," he answered. "Maybe we will start going to church."

Several weeks later the doctor's wife called Fran. "We have decided to accept Jesus Christ as our Savior," she said. "We now believe many things that we didn't before, and we're seeking to be in the will of God. We're going to start attending church, too."

After the Lord miraculously healed Fran, the surgeon saw him work in the lives of several other patients in answer to their prayers. These events helped to convince him. And ever since that doctor became a Christian, he has prayed over every patient on whom he has operated.

Yes, even as Jesus made the blind man to see in order that the work of God might be evident in his life, so he healed Fran. Many years have passed since then, and the cancer has never returned.

—*Muriel Larson*

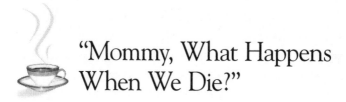

"Mommy, What Happens When We Die?"

"Ask and it will be given to you; seek and you will find; knock and the door will be opened to you."
Matthew 7:7, NIV

He was a curious four-year-old, full of questions, my son Chase. My answers usually led to more questions in his effort to understand things—all things. So the day that he tearfully gazed upon his lifeless turtle, Tommy, for the last time, Chase asked me, "Mommy, what happens when we die?"

I muttered something about our souls going to heaven, the same vague explanation I had received as a child. Although I didn't understand it back then (and I still don't), I was hoping my curious child would be content with that. But my feeble attempts to comfort and convince him were futile.

With tears spilling down his cheeks, Chase lovingly wrapped Tommy in white tissues. I lifted the lid of the red checkbook box, waiting both for Tommy's shell to be laid inside, as well as the question I knew was coming but dreaded: "Mommy, what's a soul?"

Setting the box down, I quickly grabbed the hand shovel and feverishly stabbed at the hard ground. "Oh, uh . . . it's your spirit," I mumbled, knowing full well such an answer would only lead to more questions.

As Chase lovingly patted the last handful of soil into a small mound with his tiny, dirt-stained hands, I hugged Chase and promised myself I'd get some answers—for him.

But as the days went by, and Chase asked fewer and fewer questions about death, my own questions seemed to multiply. I couldn't stop thinking about it. What really does happen after we die?

I dug out my King James Bible. I had received the Bible as a gift from my parents when I was a child, and I used it primarily to store mementos such as pressed flowers and special letters. Rarely had I actually read it.

As I flipped through the pages, all the "thees" and "thous" only frustrated me—probably the reason I'd seldom read it.

When Sunday arrived, I rolled out of bed knowing what I had to do. As a teenager I had attended church services regularly and had a longing to be near God. But as an adult, I had lots of excuses not to go—mainly wanting to sleep in. But this Sunday morning was different. I couldn't sleep. I felt driven to get up and go to one of our local churches.

I shared my plans with my husband, Chuck. "Sure, honey," he said with a look of surprise. "I'll watch the kids for an hour. Go on and enjoy yourself."

During the short drive through the quaint village of Pataskala, Ohio, I fought the butterflies in my stomach and the growing temptation to turn the car around. "What am I afraid of?"

Arriving at the church parking lot, I finally mustered up the courage to force myself out of the car and into the old brick building, quietly slipping into one of the wooden pews in the back. I fully expected to walk in, get my answer, be content, and resume life as normal.

But sitting there alone in the pew, something unexpected began to happen. As a child, all I'd heard at church was about Hell and damnation. If we sinned, we would go to hell, period. As an adult, I assumed God was mad at me for sins, such as my failed first marriage, and would never forgive me. I felt unworthy to be in God's house. I was afraid of his rejection.

But this church had a kind, elderly pastor, who seemed to stare straight into my soul as he talked about a woman at a well that Jesus visited for a drink of water. Like me, she too had been married before—not just once, but five times! Jesus knew all about her past and her present situation—even that she was not married to the man she was currently living with. Also, because she was both a Samaritan and a woman, Jesus was not supposed to be talking to her. I was amazed to hear that Jesus had knowledge of her past, yet had compassion on her and even offered her a drink of his water—living water.

Still seeming to stare directly at me, the pastor continued. "And Jesus is aware of everything you have done, too. Instead of condemning you, though, he invites you to drink of the living water that can only come from Him. That is, when you ask Jesus to forgive you and come into your life, not one but two wonderful things will happen. Jesus, through the power of the Holy Spirit, will come into your heart to love you and help you in this life. Then, after you take your last breath here on earth, the Bible says you will immediately be in the Lord's presence and spend eternity with Him in Heaven."

The pastor went on to quote from John 3:16: "For God so loved the world that he gave his one and only Son, that whoever believes in him shall not perish but have eternal life."

Perched on the edge of the pew, trying to absorb all I'd just heard, I suddenly began to sense the presence of something or someone beside me and surrounding me. It lovingly wooed me, tugging at my heart—almost as though it wanted to take up residence there. Even though there was no one else sitting with me on that pew, I knew with certainty I was not alone. God was gently nudging me to make Him my best friend.

When I returned home, I again dug out my old King James Bible with renewed vigor. Miraculously, it was beginning to make sense, especially the book of John.

John 7:37-39: "'If anyone is thirsty, let him come to me and drink. Whoever believes in me, as the Scripture has said, streams of living water will flow from within him.' By this, he meant the Spirit, whom those who believed in him were later to receive. Up to that time the Spirit had not been given, since Jesus had not yet been glorified."

I didn't ask Jesus to forgive me that day and come into my heart. I still had too many questions. Yet God, in his way and in his time, eventually answered every question that stood in the way of my doing just that. It was the beginning of the most wonderful relationship of my life—this life and the next!

—*Connie Sturm Cameron*

In the Driver's Seat of God's Love

My fifteen-year-old son was a nervous wreck. He'd failed the written test for his learner's permit twice now, and he'd developed a mental block about his abilities that seemed insurmountable. The expectations of his friends, parents, and teachers weighed heavily on his mind. Even his younger brothers, now twice denied their celebratory meal at Burger King and demanding their hamburgers and French fries, added to the load he carried. As much as he wanted to pass that test because he longed to drive, now it appeared he sought success more for others' benefit than his own.

My son's disappointment over his first failure had been written all over his face. He knew better than to try to express it with his voice. But body language is often more expressive than words, and he communicated his heartbreak with every step, the way he slouched in his seat in the car, and his steady, unseeing stare out the car window. I knew without asking that he didn't want to talk about it.

When he did speak, his words broke my heart. "I'm sorry," he said, as if he had wronged me somehow with his inability to drive the car home. "Do you think Dad will be mad?"

"No, honey," I answered, surprised at the question. "Disappointed, sure, but not *in* you . . . only *for* you." As his parents, we wanted him to drive only because he wanted to. We watched him slowly count off the months until he was fifteen and a half, the anticipation growing as the day came ever closer. And now that it had finally arrived, it floored me that he was more worried about our disappointment than his own.

Our perspectives are so different. He sees today more than tomorrow, so this failure in his present world looms large. We, on the other hand, having traveled the same road ourselves, see his todays in light of his tomorrows, thus causing his present difficulties to shrink in magnitude. We know that he will eventually drive. He doesn't have to do it today. And he never has to do it to earn our love.

Perhaps it's this same difference in perspective that makes our spiritual failures loom larger than life to us, while they bother our heavenly Father much less. He sees what we will eventually become; thus our current struggles in reaching our potential trouble Him less than they do us. His disappointment lies more in the pain we cause ourselves and in the delay in realizing our destinies than in any lessening of his love for us.

I tried to explain to my son that I loved him as much after he failed the test as I would have if he had passed it. His score didn't affect my love for him in the least, because that love is not based on his performance. He has my heart because of whom he is—a human being, my son—not what he does.

Spiritually speaking, surely we'd feel less pressure to perform for God and those around us if we would from time to time reaffirm our understanding that nothing we can do will make God love us more or less. He loves us, period. Regardless of the magnitude and repetitive nature of our sins, he knows that we have the ability, through Him, to get past the difficulties that trip us up along the way. Much as we like to please fellow Christians around us, we don't have to succeed at everything the first time we try it in order to be a hit with God. We'll find it's a whole lot easier to serve Him in whatever task He's asked of us once that pressure, which binds our ability to perform, is removed.

Just ask my son. He took his test again today. And this time he passed. We celebrated today's victory, but he was a winner in my eyes, long, long before that.

—*Elaine L. Bridge*

God Reads E-Mail

On a Sunday morning I sat at my computer checking my e-mail. I opened my mailbox, and as usual, there were at least twelve forwarded messages. They were all from the same person. Day after day I received messages like these. Most of them contain forwarded prayers—the ones that say, "If you love the Lord, you will pass this on." Others are junk. I do love the Lord, but I doubt He's going to strike me dead if I don't forward these e-mails. I couldn't imagine someone having so much time on their hands to spend the day forwarding those annoying, silly e-mails. How ridiculous! Delete, delete, delete! I had way too much to do to sit there and scroll down through endless strings of e-mail addresses and computer codes to find the actual text of each of those messages. As much as I detested these e-mails, I didn't have the heart to tell my Internet friend that they were unwanted and very irritating. So I continued to receive and delete them without opening.

Around 7:00 P.M. I had finished most of my online work, so I decided to turn the computer off and give it a rest. At 7:30 P.M. the phone rang. I didn't recognize the number on the caller ID, but I answered it anyway. An unfamiliar male voice asked, "Are you Evelyn's mother?" I replied, "Yes?" with a question in my voice. "You don't know me, but Evelyn has been working for me occasionally, and I haven't seen or heard from her for four days," he said. It wasn't unusual for me not to see Evelyn, sometimes for weeks, but she normally kept in touch with her friends.

Evelyn became addicted to drugs when she was twenty-five years old. I always knew when she was using them, because she avoided family until she was straight. I gained custody of her beautiful children, and even though she'd stay gone for weeks, she usually kept in touch by phone. This was not at all like her.

I began to cry on the phone. I hung up and started calling her friends, her roommate. No one else had seen or heard from her in four days either.

But the worst news was yet to come.

I began to get stories about some of the drug dealers. They were calling Evelyn a snitch. Apparently someone had seen her getting into a police car, and they thought she told the police everything she knew. There was no telling what these people might do (or already had done) to her. I immediately called the city police. The investigator became very concerned for Evelyn, knowing what kind of people she was dealing with, and came right over to take a missing persons report.

I was shaking and crying, but I managed to gain control before he arrived. He appeared in fifteen minutes, paperwork in hand. I hesitated as I tried to remember Evelyn's birthday. "Why can't I remember my own child's birthday?" I asked myself. Maybe because I still thought of her as my little girl. Just yesterday, it seemed, she was only fifteen, living at home, and going to school. Life was not perfect, but we were happy until some no-good jerk offered her that first illegal drug. Now her life was destroyed, and her whole family was suffering with her. Worse than that, she could be lying hurt or dead somewhere, the result of retaliation by these dealers. I too knew what kind of people they were. I myself had been to a few front doors, begging Evelyn to come home. They are not the type of people you cross. They are dangerous, heartless people who make their living killing others with drugs.

I finally blurted out the information the investigator needed. "Dear God," I prayed silently, "please, please bring Evelyn home safely." The investigator stated that he was off-duty in fifteen minutes but would stay on long enough to file the report and check some places to see if he could locate her. I thanked him tearfully and slowly went back inside.

I paced the floor until early morning, clutching the phone, waiting for any kind of word about Evelyn's whereabouts. Nothing came. I tried to sleep, but that was useless. No mother can rest when her child is missing. No matter how old the child is, she's still your baby, and you worry until the day you die. I finally managed to cry myself to sleep for an hour.

When I woke up, I called the police department. "Nothing yet," the woman replied, "but if we find her, you'll be the first to know." My heart sank again as I searched for recent pictures of her in case we had to make missing-person flyers. I couldn't find any recent photos, so I got on the Internet to contact my youngest daughter. I knew she had more recent photos and would e-mail them to me so I could print them.

I opened my mailbox, and there were another five forwarded messages from that bothersome woman. "Oh, no, not now!" I said to myself. I began to delete them one by one but stopped at the last one. I thought, "I know that prayer works. If I send an Internet prayer request to this person, I *know* she'll forward it."

I began to compose a message to tell the message-sender that my daughter had been missing for five days now, to please pray for her safe return, and to forward the e-mail to all of her friends. Within a few minutes I began to get e-mails of concern and sympathy. Within one hour of sending out my Internet prayer request, Evelyn's roommate called. "I just heard from Evelyn, and she's fine!" she said excitedly. I got on my knees and thanked God for finding her. I knew this was no coincidence! I also thanked Him for those annoying forwarded messages.

Evelyn is safe at home now, but she has a long road to recovery. She has tried many times to break this horrible addiction, but somehow she always seems to slip up. I've tried everything in my power to convince her to get help. So far nothing has worked.

I think I'll send another Internet prayer request…

After all, I know God reads e-mail.

—*Connie R. Smith*

Prescription for Rest: Remember the Sabbath

Living in the land of the free can have its disadvantages. I was born in the 1950s, and as I grew, so did the concept of a twenty-four-hour, seven-days-a-week world. Thanks to technology, I can now go to the bank, shop, work a part-time job using a personal computer, wash clothes, and go out to eat whenever I want to. Yet, instead of these abilities giving me a sense of freedom and more leisure time, I often feel compelled to keep going and pause less.

When I was younger, I wasn't allowed to play records, cards, or generally be loud on Sunday. I thought that was boring. I concluded that whoever made "blue laws" was just trying to outlaw fun. Now, however, I see that my parents were helping my siblings and me exercise a divine mandate. They were forcing us to wind down and *rest*—attend Sunday school as a reminder of God's love and goodness, read the comic strips, play board games with the family, and go for rides in the countryside while eating ice cream sundaes. What overscheduled adult or child today wouldn't do well to take the time for those things?

Today we work six or seven days a week, often long past "normal" business hours. We fill in any free time in our schedules with our modern-day ideas of fun, which can be just as exhausting as our work! A laptop computer—even the latest model—will stop running if the battery is never recharged, you can count on it. Land never allowed to be dormant will eventually stop yielding plants and crops—that's a fact. My mind and body are no different. They need rest. Instead of the technology age giving me more time for true leisure, I seem to have less.

The concept of the *Sabbath* (meaning rest) is as old as creation. Genesis 2:2 reads, "And on the seventh day God ended his work which he had made: and he rested on the seventh day from all his work which he had made." He stopped to reflect on the goodness of his creation as an example for his creatures to follow. Because he knew that on our own we would not choose to stop, rest, and reflect on the blessings in our lives, God made it a law. It's right up there with no stealing, lying, or adultery, and respecting parents and honoring God, so it must be important.

I had an epiphany on the matter of Sabbath rest one Sunday morning while standing in a supermarket checkout line. As I watched the hustle and bustle around me, more than feeling guilty about having possibly broken God's law to rest and worship him, I felt I had somehow cheated myself by not getting a heavenly prescription filled. I told my girlfriends to count me out of all Sunday shopping. They probably thought I was being fanatical about an ancient rule that has no merit for twenty-first-century independent women. Nevertheless, they were resigned. My reasoning was simple: whatever I couldn't work for, shop for, acquire, or accomplish in six days, certainly it could wait one more day for me to get back to it.

It was hard at first to spend several Sunday morning hours in complete silence, but I forced myself to do it. The stillness was somewhat eerie. My world is normally full of noise. But instead of jumping out of bed and turning the television or radio on, now I simply lie there and enjoy the quiet or the sound of birds singing. I'm not rushed as I begin my day and prepare to worship with others. When I come home from church, I lounge on the daybed listening to the radio or watching Christian television programming or documentaries on public television.

My Sunday Sabbath became so good for me that I've started stretching it into Saturdays whenever I can. I scan my personal calendar looking for Saturdays that are empty—no meetings, no seminars, no outings. Those are all good things I enjoy, but every now and then I like an entire weekend with no agenda. I wake up and simply stay in the bed and read or pray longer than usual. Then, instead of rushing through housework because I have to go somewhere, I do it leisurely while listening to gospel CDs and old R & B albums. I cook and divide up whatever I prepare into small plastic containers and freeze it to take to work for lunch—better for my pocketbook and waistline. I've lost weight because healthy food is at my fingertips. I also feel satisfied, so that relieves the temptation to buy junk food during the day. The weekdays always require a quick shower, but Saturday is my time for a bubble bath.

My friends started commenting about how much I liked to lay around on the weekend. I was offended at first because I thought they were implying I was lazy. I decided that was the real problem. As soon as you start taking blocks of time to enjoy staying in your home, spending your time reading, singing, praying, calling extended family members on the phone, and mending clothing, you are called lazy or reclusive because you're not "out there, enjoying life."

"I can't believe you don't have anything [important] to do. I am *so* busy," I was told more than once. But I do have something of significance to do. What is more vital than refreshing the spirit and renewing the mind? I guess that's why God put Sabbath rest in his ten commandments. It's a reminder that slaves cannot take a day off. Only free people can do that.

—*Susie M. Paige*

The Miracle Man

I parked my car at a golf course near my home in Fort Collins, Colorado, shortly after sunrise. The sky was clear and bright, birds were singing, and the foliage sparkled from a pre-dawn rain. I reveled in the fresh air, sunshine, and solitude, thanking God for such a magnificent Rocky Mountain morning. But everything changed when I reached the third hole.

As I swung my driver, I lost my footing on the wet grass and hit the ground hard. When I regained consciousness, I felt severe pain in my back and realized I couldn't stand up. I was alone on the course, and I knew it could be a couple hours before I was found, so I crawled the 400 long yards to my car, dragging my clubs behind me. Somehow I managed to climb behind the wheel and drive home.

After I hauled myself into the house, I called Tari, my hazel-eyed bride of four months, at the beauty salon we co-owned and operated. "I think I ripped some muscles in my back," I told her. "Could you cancel my hair appointments for a couple of days?"

"Do you want me to come home, sweetheart?" she asked. I could hear concern in her voice.

"No, I'll be fine." The pain was intense, but I was an ex-Marine and too tough for my own good. Plus I didn't realize the extent of my injury.

Tari came home over her lunch break anyway. I was lying on the couch, chock-full of aspirin. Not wanting her to know how much pain I was in, I said, "You go on back to work, honey. I'll be okay." But when she returned at 5:30 that evening, I was lying on the floor, screaming in agony. Tari called an ambulance.

That was the beginning of a twenty-six-day hospital ordeal. At first the doctors couldn't find anything wrong and tried to send me home. But I refused to leave. The pain was so excruciating, I couldn't get out of bed. Sometimes I'd black out just attempting to turn over.

Finally, after more extensive testing, my doctor came in, his brow furrowed. "You've ruptured a disk, and it's pushing into your spinal cord," he explained. "We have to get it out right away."

They immediately wheeled me in for emergency surgery, saying, "You'll be fine, Mr. Baker. It'll take some rehab afterwards, but you'll be okay."

Several hours later, however, I awoke to the glare of bright lights above masked strangers hovering over me and peering into my face. It was like a sci-fi flick or a bad dream, yet I could tell I was still in the operating room.

"Mr. Baker, move your legs!" muffled voices demanded. I tried. "Move your right toe; move your left foot!" I couldn't move anything. Then I heard someone say, "I don't know what went wrong, but we have to operate again."

So they put me back under anesthesia and hollowed out a couple of vertebrae to give my swollen spinal cord more space. When I awakened the next time, I was in a private room. Tari was beside my bed, her face white with worry.

It wasn't long before one of the neurosurgeons marched in. "Mr. and Mrs. Baker," he announced, "You need to know Larry may be a paraplegic the rest of his life. He might never walk again."

With that, he pivoted and strode out of the room. Shocked, Tari and I just stared at each other. We hadn't had a clue I could leave the operating room paralyzed.

Our lives were changed in an instant. Besides dealing with the trauma of a severely injured husband, Tari found herself running a large salon without her business partner. One night when she came into my hospital room, I could see she was worn out. I took her hand. "Honey, you're exhausted," I said. "I love it that you're here, but I love you, and I want you to go home and get some rest."

"Are you sure?" Tari asked.

"I love you," I replied, "and yes, I think that's what you should do." So she kissed me, then left.

I will never forget that evening in the hospital. It was 8:30 or 9:00 P.M. I could hear televisions and muffled voices in the distance, people shuffling up and down the hallway. But my room was silent. I felt isolated and confined, trapped in a living nightmare. I was a lonely prisoner of my own body.

When I first became paralyzed, I was told that if I could move my toes or feet within ten days, I might have a chance to recover the use of my limbs again. Well, ten days came and went without one lower-body muscle moving. It was disheartening to know I no longer had control over my body or my life.

On top of that, earlier in the day a doctor had come in and said, "I'm sorry, Mr. Baker, but I have to take your catheter out. We've got to run some tests on your bladder." He knew the pain nerves still functioned, which made the process more than uncomfortable. After he removed the tube, the doctor added with an apologetic shrug, "We'll put this back in around 9:30 or 10:00 tonight."

I didn't want to go through that torture again, so after the doctor left I did pull-up after pull-up after pull-up on the bar over my bed, trying desperately to stimulate urination before he returned. Groaning and sweating, I worked my upper muscles over and over and over, but to no avail. The urine cup on the bed stand remained empty.

That night as I lay staring at the ceiling feeling discouraged and depressed, out of the stillness a quiet voice inside my head and my heart said, "Okay, tough guy, what are you going to do now? You've called yourself a Christian for years, but you've never put me first. You've always worked out your problems your way, handled life on your own. Yet if this hospital burned down right now, you couldn't even get out of that bed. Who are you going to turn to now?"

Suddenly I realized I had always depended on myself. Although I'd become a believer while still a teenager, I'd never let God be Lord of my life. "God, I am so sorry," I said. "Will you forgive me? I promise I'll depend on you from now on." As I felt his compassion and his forgiveness flow over me, I pleaded, "I feel so helpless and alone right now. Will you please give me a sign you're with me, that you care about me and love me?"

Instantly, I felt an urge to urinate, which I saw as an incredible miracle and display of God's love for me. I reached for the cup beside my bed, tears running down my face. Later, my neurosurgeon told me, "Out of all the steps in your amazing recovery, the biggest surprise was when your bladder began functioning again."

Rehabilitation therapy in the hospital was a daily ordeal. Every session the therapists would say, "Move your left foot, move your right foot. Wiggle your left toes, wiggle your right toes." It became routine and rhetorical. But nothing ever happened.

Then one day shortly after my bladder miracle, we were going through the usual regimen when the therapist suddenly said, "Mr. Baker, I think I saw your toe twitch!" At that moment, I knew I would walk again.

When I left the hospital fourteen days later, I was still considered a paraplegic even though I had slight movement in one foot and two toes. I had a long way to go, and no one could or would predict the outcome.

Tari was a tremendous encouragement to me during the paralysis. One night she said, "Hey, hon, we're going out to dinner." She bathed me, put my best suit on me, blow-dried my hair, and got all dressed up. Then she helped me into the car and drove to one of the nicest restaurants in town. As we pulled up, she joked, "We get to use a handicapped parking spot! I've always wondered what this feels like."

Not knowing how people would react, we rolled in with our heads held high and had a wonderful, intimate evening together. We held hands, me in my wheelchair on one side of the table and Tari in her seat on the other. She looked me in the eyes and said, "You're the best-looking guy in a wheelchair I've ever seen, Larry. I love you. This will not destroy us. It's just going to make us stronger. We'll make it through no matter what."

I was convinced I would walk again, but the medical professionals weren't as optimistic. "If it happens," they said, "it'll take at least six months." But I was determined to speed up the process. After my second physical therapy session at home, the therapist said, "You're way ahead of schedule. Since you're obviously motivated and working really hard, I trust you to continue exercising on your own. Just call if you have questions."

Thanks to the healing power of God and a lot of hard work, I went from a wheelchair to a walker, to crutches, then a cane, and finally to walking on my own within seven weeks. Hospital staff members still call me the Miracle Man.

—*Larry Baker as told to Becky Lyles*

My Day in Court

In the beginning, my prayer life was simple. I repeated the Lord's Prayer upon getting out of bed in the morning and before going to bed at night. As my faith matured and I depended on God more, my prayers became more personal and fervent. My time with God, whether spent on bended knee, prostrate, or journaling, transformed from five-minute check-ins to an hour of worship, confession, supplication, and thanksgiving. The more I lived Proverbs 3:5-6, "Trust in the Lord with all your heart and lean not on your own understanding; in all your ways acknowledge him, and he will make your paths straight," the easier it was to turn to God with all my challenges. And the day I got a speeding ticket was the day I learned that my life is not insignificant to God, even when I mess up.

As I penned my traffic court date on the calendar, I asked my husband if I needed a lawyer.

"No," he said. "When you walk into the courtroom, look for the officer who gave you the ticket."

"Why?" I asked.

"To make a deal. Too bad you don't know someone who could help you out."

"What kind of deal?" I squinted at him. "I was speeding. I have to pay the price."

"Don't admit it," he pleaded. "Our insurance will go up."

Asking for a favor was out of the question. I had broken the law—another speeding ticket. More points against my license. But as parents, we must practice what we teach. And in our household, we had just decided to change our parenting style so our children would understand that if you break rules, there are consequences. Our aim was to be respected, authoritative parents. However, my heavenly Father decided to chastise me before I began disciplining my own children.

I had received my first speeding ticket two years ago. On that bright summer day, the radio was blaring and the kids singing along. I zoomed down the narrow, winding highway, ignoring the speed limit, only to encounter a police officer standing on the yellow line pulling over lawbreakers. My heart raced. My mouth was suddenly dry. My body stiffened with shame. As we parked off to the side of the highway, my daughters asked, "What happened? Why are we sitting here?"

"I broke the law," I said, my head bowed.

"Are you going to jail?" My six-year-old asked.

"No, but I will get a ticket and have to pay a fine," I said. "It's like our new rule at home. If you leave toys scattered on the floor, they go to the Goodwill."

To my mind, God was dealing with me—reality discipline. Without hesitation, I had pled guilty and paid the fine. I even made a point of slowing down after that. Although "lead foot" was my nickname, I had no choice. When heading to scheduled appointments or meetings, I allowed myself an extra fifteen minutes.

But a year later I blew it again, while rushing to get my daughter to ballet class.

Although I respected my husband's advice about what to do with the ticket, I had to do the only thing I knew was right—call on my Lord and Savior, Jesus Christ. Before I appeared in court, I needed a blanket of prayers, so I e-mailed my prayer warriors: "Please pray the officer doesn't show up in court."

The Monday morning of my court appearance, I reached for my pocket Bible and drove to the court-house. Traffic violators, uniformed policemen, and suited lawyers filled the courtroom. I was nervous. I forgot my husband's advice. So I opened my Bible to read a comforting verse. Nestled between the pages, I found eighteen dollars. "Wow, Lord, what should I do with this?" I prayed. Buy a new pair of shoes? Suddenly my husband's voice rang in my head: *Find the officer who ticketed you.* I looked for the officer's name on the photocopied ticket. Then my eyes darted from nametag to nametag. There he was, a smiling young man with dark curly hair.

"Court is dismissed for a ten-minute recess," the judge said. "When the officer calls your name, talk with him."

I hoped the officer would be as empathetic as the judge. The police officer read my violation aloud and asked if I agreed. I did. Although he reduced the fine and the points, I was still not pleased. I boldly asked if no points was a possibility. He laughed and shook his head no. I returned to the courtroom. "Okay, Lord," I said. "I trust you. This in your hands. The officer showed up. I have to pay a fine."

As I patiently waited for the court session to begin, I noticed a uniformed officer with a familiar face. He waved. I waved back. He walked toward me.

"How are you?" the man asked.

"Good," I said, trying to remember who he was.

"What did they get you for?"

"Speeding."

He playfully tapped my hand. Then I realized I had met him at the health club. His name was George.

"Come with me," he said.

We entered the lobby, where other officers and people like me stood talking. George asked me,

"What was the officer's name?" I told him, and he said he would take care of it.

Back in the courtroom, when the judge called me, I plodded to the bench. I could forget that new pair of shoes—every speeder gets a seventy-dollar fine. All I had was twenty-five dollars in my wallet and my new-found eighteen. Personal checks weren't allowed.

By the grace of God, my fine was reduced, with no points on my license. The money stashed in my Bible was enough to pay the fine. I got my discipline, but God was merciful. Being authoritative doesn't mean being harsh. It means learning the rules and understanding the consequences of breaking them.

Later that afternoon I told my husband the verdict. He gasped. "You're lucky!"

"No, I'm blessed. It's totally God—I've got nothing to do with it."

And to ensure I obey the law, I have two little reminders who ask, "Mommy, are you speeding?"

—Angela Batchelor

Now I Cry for Joy

"It's all your fault!" Jenny screamed. "You're the reason I'm like this. If I hadn't been born in this family, if you hadn't been my mother, I wouldn't be like this!" She yanked the door open and disappeared into the night.

My fault? I covered my face as tears spilled through my fingers. "Yes, it's true," I thought. "It is my fault."

My husband, Lee, and I had known for about a year that something was wrong with our fifteen-year-old daughter. Overnight, it seemed, Jenny had developed a thin, almost boyish shape.

"Look, Mom," she said one day, holding her jeans out from her waist. "These don't fit anymore."

I laughed as she folded over the waistband. "Eleven is not your size now," I said.

But I didn't laugh when Jenny dashed into the kitchen a few days later. "I ran to the dairy and back," she said. "I'm planning to do that every day."

"But Jen, that's five miles. Why all the exercise?"

Something was wrong with Jenny, but I had no name for the problem. Then one day I was leafing through a magazine, and my attention was drawn to a picture of a girl. Her cheeks were sunken, and the look in her eyes seemed familiar. The article said she had anorexia nervosa, a disease that often afflicts young women. As I read, reality gripped me. Although I had never heard of the disease—I couldn't even pronounce its name—I knew it stalked our household.

So I took Jenny to our family doctor. After examining her, he encouraged her to eat and "be a good girl." He obviously wasn't familiar with eating disorders.

I was expecting another child at the time, and when the new baby arrived, we put Jenny's situation on hold. In a household of six children, there was no time to worry about vague problems. Besides, what could possibly be wrong with a girl who was a cheerleader, homecoming queen, and the city's Junior Miss?

Before we knew it, Jenny was ready for college. We finally felt it was time to deal with her extreme thinness. "Jenny, before you go away, Dad and I feel you should see a doctor," I said.

"No, Mom! There's no problem. Please! I'll eat. I promise." She began to cry.

Once again, we dismissed our concerns. We sent a sick girl to a college 900 miles from home. Later, as

I drove Jenny back to school after Christmas vacation, she said quietly, "Mom, I really don't want to go back."

"Oh, you'll be fine once you see your friends again," I said, dismissing her plea for help.

On campus I made an appointment for Jenny to see the school psychiatrist. After talking with Jenny and looking at her records, he said, "Your daughter is a bright, highly motivated student. Whatever problem exists, I predict it will be gone by the end of this semester."

I left the college with those words ringing in my ears. Two days later, Jenny was on the phone begging us to let her come home. We took her to a psychiatrist who identified the disease and admitted her to a hospital.

Although Lee and I didn't know it at the time, we had just embarked on a vicious journey that would take us through doctors' offices and psychiatric wards for the next thirteen years.

"How can Jenny recover from anorexia?" This was the question Lee and I often asked each other. Only now the problem included another disease—bulimia. In anorexia nervosa, the person eats little and exercises vigorously, while people suffering with bulimia eat huge amounts of food, mostly at night, then purge themselves with induced vomiting or laxatives.

The tension in our home was palpable. At mealtime we'd watch Jenny devour her meal and any other food she could lay her hands on. With cheeks bulging and salad dressing running down her face, she'd reach for another piece of bread, spread it with honey, and stuff it in her mouth. Later the rest of the family would sit mute, staring at each other as we listened to the shower running and the toilet flushing to cover the sounds of Jenny vomiting up the food.

One day Lee had had enough. After supper he told Jenny, "You're going to stop this foolishness!" And he barred the door to the bathroom.

"Please," Jenny begged. "I've got to do this!" As they struggled, she proceeded to vomit on the floor.

We never tried that again. Instead, we began to ask God for help.

"What can I do?" I asked Lee after one of Jenny's nightly eating binges. "All the mayonnaise is gone, and I planned to make a salad. The brown sugar and pudding mixes are gone, too."

With frustration equal to mine, he shouted, "Don't buy any more groceries!" In desperation, we hid food in closets, under beds, and behind books in the bookcase.

There were times when Jenny tried to control her nightly binges. I cried one evening when she handed me a pair of nylon hose. "Mom, tie my foot to the bed so I won't get up in the night and eat." She often said, "I don't want to be this way. I pray. Why doesn't God hear me?"

Our family prayed, too, and we continued to take Jenny to psychiatrists. She spent another month in the hospital. Not once during the hospitalization did she induce vomiting.

"We're over the hump," the doctor assured us when she was discharged. But one day later, Jenny was back in the old cycle of eating and purging.

Then I began noticing an occasional beer can in Jenny's car. About the same time, I read this startling fact: "People who suffer from bulimia also crave alcohol and are depressed more often." Icy fingers of fear squeezed my heart. "Jenny will destroy herself one way or the other," a voice seemed to whisper.

One evening our younger daughter received a call from a bartender in the next city. "Come and pick up your sister. Bring someone along to drive her car. She's in no condition to drive."

It was then that Lee and I made the most difficult decision of our married life: we asked Jenny to move out on her own. I cried as I helped her pack her belongings. "How will she pay rent and buy food?" I asked Lee. He had no answer.

The phone rang one morning after Jenny moved out. "Mom? This is Jenny." Her voice sounded hollow. "I have nothing to live for. I'd be better off dead."

My head pounded as I considered the implication of her words. "Jenny, you must get help." My mind quickly ran through a list of people who might help.

I pounced on one name. "There's a chaplain where I work. Why don't you call him?"

Two days later Jenny called me. "I saw the chaplain. He said we're not perfect people, none of us. That's why we need God's help. All the time I tried to be so good. When I wasn't, I thought, 'What's the use of trying?'"

Life improved slightly for Jenny. She continued to eat and purge. She was extremely thin, and at times she drank heavily. But she assured me, "I'm doing the best I can." She no longer talked of suicide.

One day Jenny went for a routine dental examination, and her world fell apart. Although he didn't know she had an eating disorder, the dentist said, "I can see that you have bulimia. When you purge, the gastric juices eat away the enamel on your teeth. The enamel on the inside of your teeth is very thin. I hope I can save them."

Jenny asked me to meet her at the mall. Soberly she said, "If I lose my teeth, I'll kill myself." In the middle of the mall, we held hands and cried. The old feelings of hopelessness gathered on the horizon as I prepared for the worst.

This time Jenny turned to the Bible. "God says he will restore what the cankerworm and locust destroy," she said. "Can I ask God to heal my teeth when I'm the one who ruined them?"

"Healing is a gift," I said. "Yes, you can ask God to heal your teeth." Soon afterward the dentist began treatments to preserve the thinned enamel.

Every day was a struggle as Jenny tried to relearn normal eating patterns. Often she slipped back into the old habit of gorging and purging. I stood by, cheering her on better days and praying—on good days and bad.

With encouragement, tears, and prayers, Jenny worked toward physical, mental, and emotional healing. One day she said, "Things are shaky, Mom, but God and I together, we're going to make it. Keep praying!"

Prayer. I think of the nights of prayer, the pain, the struggles. Prayer for Jenny has drawn me closer to God. Lee and I have learned to trust him more. In those times, I cried for Jenny, for us. But now I cry for joy.

—*Jewell Johnson*

What I Learned
from a Pony

Ants, eagles, doves, sheep, and snakes. My childhood had been filled with Bible stories about these creatures. God used ants to illustrate industry, eagles to convey unlimited possibilities, doves to teach gentleness. He compared humans to sheep, and we all know who the snake represents. Now, later in life, I was about to learn a lesson from another of God's creatures.

It began when my good friend Jacque acquired a new Welsh pony named Savannah. I was intrigued by the prospect of a close-up encounter with this untrained yearling because I had not been around live animals much. I'd had one unsuccessful experience with a sandy-colored cocker spaniel, which was soon banished by my mother to the country where he could happily dig up someone else's plants. I had also ridden horses on summer vacations on the farm. But those were just rather large beasts that plodded up the road and then charged back with me clinging to the saddle. In my ignorance, I formed the idea that Jacque was getting herself something like a large teddy bear—a cute, cuddly plaything.

When Jacque called a few days after Savannah's arrival, the tension in her voice accompanied a tale of high drama. The adorable pony with the appealing eyes was proving feisty and downright obstinate. Whenever Jacque approached her with the halter, Savannah turned and ran to the opposite corner of the field.

After Jacque finally caught her, Savannah took an instant dislike to her stall. She whinnied, reared high, and thrashed about. Jacque tried everything she knew to calm the wild-eyed, angry pony, but nothing worked. In a desperate attempt to escape, Savannah threw both front hooves against the stall bars—and one hoof got jammed. Frenzied, she tried to wrench her leg free as Jacque watched in horror. She could almost hear Savannah's tiny bones snap.

"Oh, God, please help me!" Jacque cried. With extreme care, she began pushing the large hoof through the narrow space while Savannah snorted and struggled on the other side of the bars. It was hopeless. The only solution seemed to be a tranquilizer shot. Jacque ran to the house. Syringe in hand, she tore back to the barn and screeched to a stop at the sight before her. A free and somewhat cowed Savannah stood on the far side of the stall, inspecting her surroundings. Jacque examined the bent bars. Nobody but a guardian angel could have freed Savannah's hoof without damage.

When I visited Jacque, I went down to the pasture gate to view this "wild beast" that was such a headache. There she stood, calmly tearing the good grass Jacque had planted. Her large brown eyes turned in my direction and gave me a cursory glance.

Over the next two years, I observed Savannah's progress with interest. I learned what goes into the physical care of a pony, the dedication and commitment required of the caregiver. Her mane had to be cut, pulled, and combed. A farrier regularly trimmed her hooves. While I lay snug in bed, Jacque ventured out into many cold, rainy nights to bring Savannah into shelter. The pony's coat grew thick and shiny from a balanced diet. I often watched Jacque bathe and brush her, then spray her with fly repellent. Or, with a tender touch, she would spread soothing ointment on a wound or bite.

My mind reflected on all those Sunday school stories where I learned about God's care for his children. Was it possible that God invested as much effort in my care as Jacque was doing for Savannah? A concept formed before my eyes.

Initially, it took every ounce of Jacque's expertise in training ponies to communicate to Savannah "who da boss!" Savannah ran away when called, deliberately kicked over her water trough, and generally let Jacque know about her displeasure. She despised Jacque's rain jacket and reacted with drama whenever the "dreaded poncho" approached, snatching at it and trying to rip it off. With patience and skill, Jacque worked with Savannah, praising her when she was good, withholding meals when she wasn't, reading her moods, identifying what made her happy and what triggered rebellion. Savannah hated being brought into her stall to eat, and there were many battles of will down by the pasture gate. Sometimes Jacque's treatment seemed harsh; the discipline severe. But she continued to draw on her instincts and experience.

Gently, she moved toward the goal of getting Savannah to trust her, to recognize that her underlying intentions were for Savannah's good. Time passed, and it gradually dawned on me that more was going on with Savannah than providing for her physical well-being. Jacque did not buy Savannah to be a teddy bear. Savannah's blood lines held promise that she could become an excellent competitive pony. Jacque talked about the potential that flickered in her on occasion.

For the first time, I began to grasp the distinction between a caregiver and a nurturer. A caregiver takes responsibility for providing for physical needs. A nurturer functions on a deeper level, looking beyond the visible. There is an emotional investment independent of care giving.

As I watched Jacque in her combined yet distinctly different roles of caregiver and nurturer, a thought came to me. Can the idea of God as caregiver and protector be expanded to encompass nurturing? Being nurtured was a foreign concept to me. I received excellent physical care as a child, but the essence of who I was shriveled through benign neglect. Could I accept belated nurturing from someone with the power to resurrect the ebbing life inside me? I wondered if God read me as Jacque "reads" Savannah. By remaining constantly alert to ways of connecting with the animal, Jacque discovered how much the pony loved her creature comforts. This became a means of communicating, the foundation to building a relationship. In all the ups and downs of training, Jacque meticulously avoided doing anything that might crush Savannah's spirit.

Two years later, the untrained, stubborn youngster in Jacque's care was gone. In her place is a beautifully maturing pony that shows signs of fulfilling her destiny. Other than the occasional expression of displeasure, Savannah happily obeys her master's commands. Each morning she waits at the gate for Jacque to appear. She is then led into a clean stall to drink cool water, munch on sweet hay, and snooze under a whirring fan through the heat of a summer's day. Her level of trust has risen to the point where she almost resents Jacque disturbing her rest time, getting lazily to her feet while Jacque gently brushes the wood shavings from her face and ears.

Now when Jacque puts the halter over her head, Savannah lingers a little while, waiting for her ears to be rubbed, anticipating some loving strokes. Instead of snapping at Jacque's poncho, Savannah nuzzles the sleeve with her lips. Nurturing accomplished in Savannah what mere care giving could not. It brought out the best in her and prepared her to fulfill what her breeding designed her to become. She now shows a key trait—amazing patience with small children and dogs. There is only the merest hint of annoyance when Harry, the Welsh corgi, hangs on her tail. A special bond of trust formed between trainer and trainee.

As Jacque worked with Savannah, I opened myself to a deeper level of God's care. My will frequently collided with his, but like Jacque with Savannah, God looked beyond my willfulness and rebellion and saw my potential. With immeasurable patience, he waited for my trust in Him to build. When I wanted to go tearing off in the wrong direction, I felt a gentle tug on my reins. Serendipitous blessings meant to me what tender carrots did to Savannah. Not pushing or rushing, God worked at convincing me he desired the best *for* me and was committed to doing everything necessary to bring out the best *in* me. And always, there was that insistent whisper, urging me to venture forth into discovering who God designed me to be.

I recently watched Jacque as she worked with Savannah. Everything about the pony communicated exuberance and pleasure. Savannah enjoyed showing off what she was capable of doing. Pride and deep satisfaction shone out of Jacque's eyes as she saw how Savannah had blossomed.

The Creator is a master at balancing care giving and nurturing. Like Savannah, I am benefiting from both.

—*Joy Wooderson*

The Evil of Conformity

I rescued a prayer book from a secondhand bookstore earlier this year. Much like my mother's prayer book that I carried at my wedding, this one was filled with prayers from the early days of the Christian church. At the back, however, was an additional writing simply titled "Rules for a Godly Life." This piece was what I found interesting. There was one phrase that really jumped out at me, and although it was only four words, it spoke volumes about an issue I wrestle with almost daily: "Evil companions demand conformity."

It's funny, you don't hear a lot about evil these days. Only now the term has been thrown around in the media regarding recent world events. But we need to realize that the broad-scale evil in such instances began with small-scale evil operating on an individual level, demanding that other individuals conform to it.

We do live in a world that demands conformity. Let's face it—if you want to succeed by worldly standards, you have to conform to its ideals. To get ahead, you have to look out for yourself, get in with the right people, and go with the flow of the crowd. If you don't at least tip your hat to the social politics that govern us, you are ostracized, and suddenly the crowd is working against you. The interests of a few determine the destiny of the whole—and I have always had a problem with this.

I was never one to run with the crowd. If there is a label that describes me, it's *nonconformist*. To me, a real friend is somebody you like and trust for whom they are, not for what they can do for you. This simple belief has made me an outcast. In high school, I was chastised for being friends with people from so many "outside" groups instead of sticking with one clique. In college, people turned away when I wouldn't allow them to tell me how to run my life. Even now in the workplace, I am considered strange because of my refusal to put myself and a small group of individuals above the needs of the many. One thing I've learned in my time on this earth is that no matter where you go, there is always somebody trying to put you down.

It is a lesson we are wise to learn young. If you think you can get away from the demand for conformity, you are wrong. It is at every school, workplace, and any other organization where more than one person gathers. No matter where you go, there will always be groups of people that run the show based on their personal interests. It has always been there and will never go away. The best interest of the group is always compromised by the special interests of a few.

I came to accept a long time ago that I will never belong to this kind of world. I have actively chosen to accept God's grace through Christ's salvation, and I will live my life with integrity and honesty. My goal is not to achieve worldly success but to do what God sent me into this world to do, which is help as many people as possible. If the world sees it as wrong, then I will just be wrong. God made each of us unique, for a unique purpose, and we are all free in Christ to be who we are and serve that purpose. I fully believe that "by the grace of God I am what I am, and his grace toward me was not in vain" (1 Corinthians 15:10). I will not hurt people in order to be popular or to move ahead in life. In my heart, that is no success at all. That is betrayal.

I have paid the price for holding to my standards. I could have seen more worldly success in my life if I would just go with the flow, but the price was too high to pay. I refuse to sacrifice my devotion to living a godly life, to my family, my friends, or the people I serve through my work for selfish interests. Real progress comes through personal growth, and real success comes through service to other people. I want to continue to grow in maturity and wisdom through Christ, and to use this growth to help and serve other people with honesty and integrity. Those virtues are worth more than any promotion or amount of money in this world.

There is nothing wrong with me or with anybody else who chooses not to follow the crowd. In reality, nobody has the right to judge anybody else, yet that doesn't stop people from doing it anyway. It is an age-old problem. Paul even rebuked the Romans for this behavior, asking them, "Who are you to pass judgment on the servant of another? It is before his own master that he stands or falls. And he will be upheld, for the Master is able to make him stand" (Romans 14:4). If you know and accept this truth, it doesn't matter what "the crowd" says about you because their gossip is useless. Let them talk—they never stop talking anyway.

I accept the fact that I will always stand on the outside. I don't have to be squeezed into the world's mold because I don't belong to this world. In fact, if refusing to conform to society makes me a renegade, then I'm ready to shatter their perfect world by living up to a higher standard. I'm not afraid to pay the price, and you shouldn't be either. Stand tall and fight the evil demanding your conformity! You are a child of God, and you are free to be whom he made you. If you ever feel alone, remember: No matter how big the crowd seems, there are always more outsiders than insiders, so you have plenty of company.

Conformity is a prison that never allows you to be the person God made you to be. To go against conformity is to claim true freedom.

—*Sherri Fulmer Moorer*

I Have Seen Him

Three times in my life I have waited through endless days and bottomless nights while someone I love fought for life in an Intensive Care Unit (ICU).

We lost the first battle in 1970. My sixteen-year-old sister, Debbie, lost control of our father's car and hit a tree; she was pinned between the steering wheel and the side door. Her ribs were crushed, puncturing both lungs. In the hospital, she was completely conscious but unable to talk or move around because of the respirator and drainage tubes in her chest.

According to ICU rules, Debbie was only allowed one short visit every two hours, but because she was so alert and frightened, the kind nurses let our mother sit with her several hours a day. Exhausted, Mama would keep up a cheerful front, singing to Debbie and sharing news about the family, everything except how badly she was hurt.

By the fifteenth day, the only song Debbie wanted to hear Mama sing was "Jesus Loves Me." Later that evening, she left us.

Seven years later, it was just as wrenching, but my ten-month-old niece was healed. Cristy had been plagued for months with persistent chest congestion, coughing, and high fevers. Finally, Cristy's doctor put her in the hospital to receive stronger antibiotics and intravenous fluids. But instead of improving, she continued to get worse until she was moved to Intensive Care in critical condition with viral pneumonia. The sight of that little darling, with drainage tubes and a respirator in her chest, so much like Debbie had been, just about did all of us in. With every labored breath that Cristy drew, we relived Debbie's agony and our loss.

For nearly a month, Cristy lay unresponsive as doctors fought to save her. Then, miraculously, she began to recover. Within a few days of leaving intensive care, she was the same bubbly toddler she'd been before.

My third nightmare in the ICU came in 1996. This time it was my own daughter, our beautiful Karyn, now 25, who lay attached to chest tubes and a respirator, and monitors of every description. They said it was a miracle she had lived long enough to get to the hospital after a pickup truck rolled over her Toyota.

Doctors were blunt: Karyn was unconscious from a closed head injury and would not live through the night.

But she did. As the hours of darkness turned into day, and then another day, the prognosis didn't change. Karyn simply could not live with the kind of brain damage she had sustained.

Now I was the mama at my daughter's bedside, singing and making cheerful conversation while my heart pounded in terror. Blinking lights and beeping monitors proved scientifically that Karyn's heart was beating, but she responded to nothing. With both Debbie and Cristy, the doctors had tried to hold out hope for us. But with Karyn, they offered no such hope. They didn't believe she would live.

As the days and weeks passed, it became apparent that Karyn had survived her accident. But her prognosis went from worst possible to unimaginable: Her doctor told us she would never come out of the coma.

Six weeks after her accident, Karyn left the hospital. But this time we had neither the finality of death, with its hope of heaven, nor the blinding joy of healing and restoration. Karyn was neither alive nor dead, but trapped in that netherworld somewhere in between. She was moved to another hospital, one experienced in coma stimulation. Her doctors still told us that she would not wake up.

Then it got worse.

Four months after the accident, the doctors told us Karyn might come out of the coma but would likely not be able to move or speak, hear or see. If she woke up, we might not even know it.

I found Hell that day—and it *is* a place. It's a dim room with a shell of a child, head and limbs tied upright into a wheelchair, body twisted into impossible contortions, and eyes void of life. I sat on the floor at Karyn's feet, looking up into the face of this pitiful stranger who used to be my daughter. And I began to imagine painless methods for us to escape this living hell.

Then in the black pit, the fiery agony of that day, I found hope. It was only a flicker, kindled so deep inside me that it might have gone out. But, like Karyn, against all reason it lived. I found hope lying on a grey metal cabinet by Karyn's bed. It was a small white card from a stranger. It simply said, "Dear Karyn, I am still praying for your recovery." It was one of hundreds, some from family, some from friends, and some, like this one, from someone who had never met us. She wanted us to know that after four months, she had not forgotten. After four months—more than 120 days—she still lifted up Karyn's name to our heavenly Father in prayer.

Five months after her accident, Karyn began to rouse from her coma—not in a glorious burst of consciousness, but rather as if she were trapped in a dark cave and feeling her way out. One day she cried out in pain, on another she laughed, and on another she watched me walk across her room. Then one day, we put a keyboard in her lap, and she typed these words, with one crooked finger: "I love."

Today, eight years later, Karyn is no longer a social worker with a husband and a career. But she is a poet and a philosopher. She spends her days corresponding over the Internet, offering encouragement and insight into issues like religion and politics, poverty, and child abuse, with friends all over the world. Her wheelchair offers silent testimony to the physical changes she has undergone, she often forgets her nurse's name, and her halting speech is difficult to understand. But her fine mind, her quirky sense of humor, her childhood memories, her love for her family, and her faith in God live.

People often marvel that our family has been through so much. They tell us that we are to be commended for keeping our faith, no matter what, that Karyn would be healed. But I was there. And I know it was not our faith that helped us through losing Debbie or that healed Cristy or that brought Karyn back to us. During those times in my life, I could not pray because of the choking fear that swallowed me; it was the prayers of other people that God heard. People who dared to ask him for what they wanted, and what they knew we wanted. Good people who understood when I couldn't find my own faith and who stood in the gap, never criticizing, but interceding for me, for my family, and for the wounded people we loved. People who remembered, day after day, week after week, month after month, to pray for us, even when their own lives and the problems they faced claimed their attention.

In each of these desperate times, God chose to answer those prayers differently. I don't pretend to know why, but I realize now that I don't have to know. What I do know is this: that God is always God, in the bad times and the good. And as long as we can see him in the faithfulness of his people, he will never be invisible. And yes, I have seen him.

—*Linda Darby Hughes*

Following God's Lead

Submission. This word strikes fear into the very heart of many modern-day women. It conjures up visions of weak-willed wives who let their husbands walk all over them—women who have no voice in their marriage and no life of their own. This is what I believed when my husband and I first took our marriage vows. The Lord has since taught me the real meaning of submission, and I couldn't have been farther from the truth!

My mother was the kind of woman who could do anything or would at least find out how to do it. So I grew up believing that I, too, could do whatever I set my mind to, and I didn't need a man to do anything for me. Don't get me wrong—I still believe God created women to be amazingly strong people who can accomplish more than most CEOs of major corporations. But at the time, I balked at *anyone* who tried to tell me what to do. In fact, I even had a hard time accepting friendly advice or helpful guidance.

After I married, I continued in this pattern, much to my husband's dismay. He loved and respected me, so I really had nothing to fear. But I carried around my refusal to be mastered like a set of useless luggage. Whenever my husband would try to take charge in our relationship, I would recoil. "No way—no one tells me what to do!" I would think. So a pattern emerged: I was in command of the home, and my husband was in charge of his job. It wasn't until later that I learned my reaction to my husband was a response to fear—fear of losing control of my life. Funny thing was, I really didn't have control of my life: God did!

After about thirteen years of marriage, I joined a women's Bible study that was responsible for changing my views completely. My husband was taking college courses during his off-duty time from his Army job. One Wednesday morning as I was preparing for my women's group, my husband asked me if I could help him with a college paper, which was due that day. He is chronic procrastinator, so it wasn't an unusual request. Usually I would rant and rave about how he should have done this ahead of time and how he puts everyone else out by waiting until just before the deadline to finish his work. That time, however, I knew my usual response was wrong. My women's group had studied submission that past week, and I was learning to see things from God's perspective.

Before I could respond, the phone rang. It was a friend from the study group, calling to see if I would be attending that morning. I asked her advice about what I should do, and she said, according to Scripture, I should stay home and help my husband. He is my highest priority, behind God.

What? I was floored! How could she suggest that I miss the opportunity to spend time in Bible study with other women of God in order to bail my husband out of a mess he got himself into? In one single moment, my mind was transformed, and I began to see things from a view that was a complete 180 degrees from my old view. The beacon of truth shown brightly in my mind. Aha! So this is the kind of submission God wants from us! He wants us to put our husband's needs before our own and help him when he needs help.

So I stayed home and typed that paper with gusto, "as to the Lord" (Ephesians 5:22). I felt energized to know that I was submitting to my husband, for maybe the first time in our marriage! And I even finished helping him in time to make it to my Bible study, which goes to show that God wanted me there, but he was going to get me there in his time! I couldn't wait to share my revelation with my class since it perfectly illustrated our lesson for the week. As I recounted the story, the leader made a simple but profound statement: "You are not his mother."

"Well, duh," I thought. "I certainly have never treated my husband like my son." Oh, really? Then why had I felt the need to punish him for his procrastination by leaving him to fend for himself? The realization hit me like a cold splash of water. I had been treating him like my son all these years while thinking that was something *other* women did. I thought back to all the trips to the grocery store where I had observed with disgust the way some women treated their husbands, telling them to "Wait right there" and berating them for choosing the wrong cut of meat. Those men looked beaten and worn down. All those times I had said a silent prayer of thanks that I did not treat my husband in such a way and for the Lord to please let me know if I did. Well, here was the answer to that prayer! Maybe I hadn't publicly scold him, but I surely hadn't put his needs, wants, and desires before mine. I hadn't allowed him to take the lead in our family life, and I certainly had never let him forget how his weaknesses should be strengthened. I had been trying to train him in the same way a mother instructs a son. All these years I had let my fear of being dominated and of losing control of my own life lead me down a path of marital destruction. It was a path clearly separate from God's path.

During the next few weeks, I learned that the act of submitting is a choice. In fact, the meaning of the word, according to *Webster's Dictionary*, is "to surrender or yield to the will or authority of another." So submitting is actually a decision I can make—the decision to think of my husband's needs and desires ahead of my own. That actually sounded very empowering! The realization that I can decide to yield to my husband's will also felt liberating. I could know that when I make that resolution, I am following God's will for me as a wife. James 4:10 assures us that when we humble ourselves before the Lord, he will lift us up. Well, that explained why I felt like I had been set free. The Lord had lifted me up!

I can't say that I have displayed the properties of the perfect submitting wife since that discovery of two years ago. I have made many mistakes and grieved over the pain I've caused my husband over the years. But the healing God has brought to our marriage is miraculous, and we are stronger than ever. Imagine that, coming from a woman who used to feel afraid to let her husband act as the head of her family. Now I know that when he leads, God leads.

—Cindy Boose

A Well-Lit Road

Rays of sun broke through my bedroom window blinds, and I curled deeper into my bed sheets with a groan. If I could just keep everything dark, I wouldn't have to see that the road I was headed down led to nowhere.

In the three years since my senior year at Cornell University, I had amassed a record number of visits to psychiatrists, therapists, emergency rooms, and mental hospitals. Together they only landed me back where I had started, in my old bedroom at my parents' house, in no shape to face the world.

None of my doctors could agree on my diagnosis in the haze of the previous years. Depression, schizoaffective disorder, bipolar disorder. It didn't seem to matter to them that each condition they named for me carried a progressively worse stigma and its own distinct baggage.

Depression means that you pass through life in a pain-filled sleep that keeps away the darker feelings you have when awake. Bipolar, and you teeter on the edge of up and down. Schizoaffectives are unable to even decide between mood swings and psychosis, and they end up with the unhappiest mix of both.

Although I knew I needed a sense of purpose more than any medication, it was easier to be sedated and kept under watch in mental hospitals, jails, therapy sessions, and the downtown daycare center for befuddled adults with no place to go. The pills made me feel even more befuddled and unsure of why my life had veered off the track toward acceptable success and normality and crashed instead in a wasteland of no job, few friends, and the haunted feeling that there was no way out.

But on that morning, I felt something was about to change. I turned on my radio, as I always did upon waking, and listened carefully to the words. Music transformed what I thought were the singers' special messages to me into a more palatable dose. Sometimes I still grew giddy with the amazement of it all, pop singers speaking directly to me through the radio. Madonna and Michael Jackson didn't talk to just anyone, I knew. The Top 40 king and queen had singled me out for heaven knew what reason, and I didn't have the energy to figure out why.

I heard my mother's footsteps on the stairs before she appeared in my doorway. She took one look at my disheveled hair, rumpled pajamas, and the expression on my face. "Do you want me to call Donna?" she asked. "Maybe she can see you today."

I couldn't trust that the worry in her voice wasn't something else, maybe the sound of resentment that she wasn't the pop world's chosen one.

I was silent for a minute, thinking. It might be a relief to get professional counseling about whether saying Madonna's name "like a prayer" constituted a sin.

"All right." The sullenness in my voice hid my fear. I hated needing a therapist, proof that I wasn't ready to think—or live—on my own. I hated being afraid of what would become of me, forever in and out of mental hospitals, only able to work at the local Chinese restaurant on my "strong" days.

We headed downtown to the mental health clinic and sat waiting for my therapist, Donna. When a husky woman came to the door, I glanced at her limp brown ponytail and the papoose on her back. "Hi, I'm Carol Ames," she said, sticking round fingers toward me. Was this some kind of test? "Donna's on vacation, and I'm the on-call therapist."

I followed Carol into a barren room, not looking back at my mother in the lobby.

"You want to tell me what's going on?" She pushed away her son's fist from her ear.

"I've realized some things recently," I began. I stopped as her two-year-old's head popped out from behind her. He stared at me and giggled, then darted back behind his mother. I glared at the pattern of dirty-beige tiles on the floor, shifting impatiently to let Carol know I was ready to leave. After a few closed-ended questions from her and no more words from me, we both withdrew into simply sitting there, the silence growing into a wall.

"I've got to go," I said, standing up abruptly. "Thanks for your time."

I rushed through the door, fighting to stay calm. My mother stood up and looked at me.

"Did you talk about what's bothering you?"

"No!" I cried. "She had a stupid baby on her back the whole time!" I fought back tears. "I'm going for a drive."

I caught a glimpse of Carol as I was leaving. She watched me go, looking as though she had too many things to do and knew she could do nothing more.

"It's up to me," I told myself angrily. "No one else can tell me what I'm supposed to do with my life."

I sped down Interstate 81 in my red Sunbird, beckoned by the promise of calm, the green peace of trees in the Great Smoky Mountains fifty miles away. I could barely see the highway as tears welled in my eyes.

"It's too hard, God," I spoke to the windshield. "I can't live the life you want me to. It's too hard to live with passion. But I can't live with death, either. That's all I see, everyone living a numbed, blank death."

I stared at the radio, then switched it on as Madonna's voice filled the car: "When you call my name/It's like a little prayer . . ."

"Help me," I whispered. "Help me fly with you." The road became a blur of gray and white as my whole body shook with sobs. They rose up from deep inside me at the thought of help on the way, at the walls beginning to crumble after being sealed tight so long. I reached for the Kleenex box on the floor. Suddenly my car skidded on the shoulder, and I spun in a wild blur of screeching tires and the terror of losing all control. I heard my own screams, screams begging God to save my life, suddenly knowing that only he could. Then everything went black.

I was soaring above the highway. Wind rushed over my entire body as I flew, suspended in air. I could see that I was still wearing my red shirt and blue jeans and my purple Saucony running shoes. "So this is what it feels like to fly," I mused. I thought about how God was granting my longtime wish to fly, but my heart felt hollow. Shouldn't I feel joy?

A terrible loneliness hit me then, and I feared that this loneliness would be my final sentence. There were no other people around me, only the cars crawling down below, the highway, an overpass. All of them were oblivious to me, my identity quickly forgotten. This was worse than the isolation I'd found living among others. This was a terrible place, where I'd never see another human again. "I don't want to fly anymore," I thought desperately. "Please, please, let me stop flying."

In an instant, I was back in the driver's seat of my Pontiac, behind a shattered windshield. A man with sandy-colored hair passed and turned to look as I yelled at him, "Help! Help me!" His distress had an odd look, and he kept on walking, past the front of my car.

Angrily, I muttered, "If you won't help me, I'll help myself." I recalled a poster of starving children tacked up outside our Catholic school gym when I was in the fifth grade. All my classmates argued with me over the meaning of the block letters lining the bottom: "Heaven help us if you won't." I argued that it incorporated a kind of old-fashioned exclamation: "Heaven help us!" My classmates finally went to our teacher to find the truth. She agreed with them; only heaven could help in the last resort.

But I would have to help myself. I lifted the door handle and pushed. It wouldn't budge. Determined to do it on my own, I scooted over the parking brake lever to the passenger side, glancing down at my left pants leg, covered in blood.

Then I came to, peeling open my eyes to see the same man and a few others dressed in white uniforms looking down into my face. "The rescue squad found me?" I thought, sinking back into blackness. When I awakened again, it was to another face, a balding man with glasses was putting stitches in my forehead. I howled, but my voice sounded so far away. Then I fell unconscious once more.

The truck driver who had followed behind me told the police that my car flipped over several times, coming to rest finally in a field beside the highway. It was months before my father told me he had seen my car towed away, smashed on all sides and the top, every window shattered. He said, his voice shaking a little, "It's a miracle you survived." And only sixteen stitches. I remembered none of it. I remembered only the flying. That was what haunted me, the loneliness of the flying.

All these years, I had wanted something humongous, believing that my life meant nothing without the excitement and glamour of someone as famous as Madonna. But suddenly all that didn't matter. Madonna might have had a slice of something, but she didn't have it all. I wanted a wholly different pie. From now on I wanted to call out to God for help, not a pop singer. God was the only one who could fill the loneliness; He was the only one who knew how. I'd simply been too blind to see it.

The day I left for graduate school in the autumn of 1994, I thought of my future teaching English as a second language to immigrants making a new home in America. In some ways, their quest paralleled my own; while they settled into their new homes and new country, I found my own new center of being.

The sun shone with a warmth that made my heart beat with anticipation. I knew God had put me on a path to something exactly right for me. It wasn't the sun that had blinded me in the years before, only my egotism and belief in what others defined as success. The sun didn't shine too brightly for my taste anymore. That day, life was exactly as it was supposed to be.

—*Christine P. Wang*

Amazing Grace

The heavy metal door of the small chapel screeches open, allowing a shaft of early evening sunlight to spill suddenly into the darkened entryway. Four-part harmony wafts out of the opened door and into the silent parking lot, as two shadows make their way slowly, slowly across the threshold. Eventually the two women following the shadows, one elderly, the other young, make it into the vestibule. The people seated in the pews, intently listening to the closely braided harmonies of a men's quartet, throw a brief glance over their shoulders, then return their attention to the front. From my vantage point, seated in one of the folding chairs set up along the back wall of the sanctuary, I keep a mildly curious eye on the door and on the slow pace of the new arrivals. Then at last I recognize them—sweet Ruth and her grandma, come to hear the concert.

Ruth's grandma, Millie, is nearly eighty years old. Failing health has brought her far from her home in the Midwest to Alaska, where she now lives with her son and daughter-in-law, Ruth's parents. This evening Millie is wearing dark sunglasses. She makes her way across the entryway in a slow shuffle, each step an independent decision. Her cane, firmly gripped with her right hand, thumps out the unsteady rhythm of her ponderous progress. With her left hand, she holds on to her grown granddaughter's arm. Ruth, a steady, quiet-spirited woman in her mid-twenties, gently smiles as she keeps her eyes on her grandma.

The setting of our little chapel belongs on a calendar page. Nestled comfortably along the shore of Turnagain Arm in Anchorage, Alaska, one whole side of the small sanctuary is made of glass. The incredible creativity of God himself peers in through those windows. A curved ribbon of silvery shoreline edges the ever-changing face of the inlet. Further back from shore, majestic, craggy mountains stand hunched above the whole scene, looking over the chapel and far out to sea. At times the view seems harsh and foreboding—house-sized hunks of ice rushing ominously on the incoming tide; frigid, gale-force winds fiercely whipping the snow into a blizzard. But other times, like this particular evening, when everything is washed in low, golden light, it is as inviting as grandma's parlor on a Sunday afternoon; the clock on the mantelpiece ticking comfortingly and the fan whirring overhead. Regardless of the season or mood, that view always reminds me of just how small we all are—how needful. The view also reminds the pastor to spoon up riveting, passionate sermons, because so-so sermons would be preached to a congregation collectively turned aside, gazing out the windows.

Tonight, when the door opens for Ruth and her grandma, our little church is dressed in September's finest. The lingering hours of Alaska's abundant summer sunshine have finally spent themselves, and brisk autumn breezes laden with the sweet-and-sour scent of ripe cranberries have blown dusky twilight back to its rightful suppertime place. It's a Norman Rockwell kind of evening, one that makes you happy to belong—or wish you did.

Millie and Ruth have cleared the doorway and are heading for a nearby row of chairs as the quartet finishes their song and begins the next one, "Amazing Grace." The audience listens, heads tilted to one side, some with eyes closed.

"Amazing grace, how sweet the sound . . . "

The young men in this quartet have grown up singing together in our community. Their hard work and God-given talents have brought them some success as they have been pursuing their careers outside of Alaska the past several years. Tonight they have come home to sing for the audience that loves them best. Like Ruth, they are feeding and tending their roots, but with tendrils of four-part harmony rather than a strong, young hand firmly clasped in an elderly, weakening one.

"I once was lost, but now am found . . . "

Millie and Ruth finally arrive at two empty chairs. Ruth, eyes either on Millie or respectfully lowered, taps her toe to the music as she waits with a patience beyond her years. Millie is doing the best she can to maintain her balance, while stepping sideways into the row and sitting down. I marvel at Ruth's desire to take the time to bring her grandma to the concert and at Millie's willingness to work so hard to walk in and sit down.

" . . . was blind, but now I see."

I'm also watching another threesome, two rows ahead of me—a twenty-something son with his parents. The mother is sandwiched between her men, and all three of them are focused on the music. The son looks like a tradesman: strong, clean-cut, wearing jeans and a plaid shirt. His left arm extends protectively around his mom's shoulders and to the midway point of his dad's back. There, his muscular hand, rather than draping across his dad's chair, is grasping the back of his dad's shirt with a tough tenderness, a sweet possessiveness.

"'Twas grace that brought me safe thus far . . . "

My throat aches and tears threaten. Maybe it's the gorgeous, sentimental harmony coming from the front of the room. Maybe it's just that I miss my own mom—still living in Tennessee while I've lived, for a long time, in Alaska. At fifty, maybe I fear growing older and more needful. Or maybe I'm just awed by God's amazing grace—by the aching beauty of grown children loving their parents and grandparents with such quiet, unassuming dignity, in a little Alaska seaside chapel bathed in autumn's cranberry-scented breeze.

"And grace will see me home."

—Nancy N. Gates

The Power of Touch

Kampong Chhnang. An exotic-sounding place situated several hours by road from Phnom Penh, but we were not there for sightseeing. After submitting to a thorough search of our personals, we stepped through huge barred gates, which clanged shut behind us, and entered a different world.

Wrenched from my comfort zone and trembling with apprehension, again I wondered what I was doing here in a drab Cambodian prison. The oppressive atmosphere weighed on my soul, yet I was merely a visitor, part of a small group come to lift the spirits of the inmates for a brief hour or two.

To our interpreter, himself a former inmate of Communist concentration camps, this was familiar territory. It wasn't entirely strange to us either, having visited a Thai prison at Chon Buri the previous year. There, two thousand young men attended our concert. But it seemed to me they already possessed hope. Here, it was obvious hope didn't exist.

It is said the eyes are the windows of the soul. When we communicate with another person, we search their eyes for that glimmer of understanding, that flicker of interest, that spark of accord or dissent. We see the person inside. But the eyes of these prisoners were lifeless. I could only see fleeting sidelong glances, downcast eyes, and deadpan expressions. Their souls were as barred to human emotions as their bodies within the confines of their cells were barred from a normal life. They were crushed beings learning to survive by building barricades for protection against both the humiliation hurled from without and the ravages of guilt within.

Did they deserve to be here? Yes. Some for taking a life. Some were just in the wrong place at the wrong time. Many had been implicated in the drug culture and all that it involves. All were probably guilty of the charges against them. But that wasn't the point. We were here to offer that elusive cup of comfort.

Could they accept it?

The prison chaplain, a doctor who had given up his lucrative practice to minister to his suffering countrymen, welcomed us warmly. I felt humbled by his sacrificial attitude. We only stopped in from the big, free outside world, and soon we would fly out again. He would stay the course.

I hated the way the prison authorities yelled and bullied their charges into a neat formation before marching them in lines to an open-sided shelter absent of chairs. All were seated cross-legged, like small children, a warden parading before them, daring anyone to move. Not exactly a great atmosphere for a lead-up to our concert! I struggled against the indignity. I struggled against my own helplessness. And I struggled against the turmoil of my emotions. But as they say, the show must go on. We all felt the same way, for we carefully set our masks in place and began our performance.

Packages from World Vision were on hand for each prisoner, and though longing to distribute them immediately, we resisted, cautioned by the thought they might believe it to be some sort of bribe to gain their attention. No, we ourselves would have to earn that respect.

We offered them all that we could. The freedom to applaud or not to applaud. To laugh or remain stony-faced. They would be free to give or withhold. It wasn't much, merely "a cup of cold water" offered in Jesus' name, but it was a small triumph for us.

Guitars strummed and young singers broke into joyful songs set to haunting, rhythmic Khmer melodies. Toes wiggled to the beat—but there was no change of expression. I taught them a simple action chorus in English, this time asking for their participation. A couple of guards leaning against posts got caught up in the spirit of things and entered in, somehow signaling the prisoners to join in too. A little more unbending. More songs . . . and this time, forgetting themselves, they clapped along.

The chaplain prayed. I couldn't understand a single word, but he poured out his heart and soul into that passionate prayer. The prisoners were silent, as in a holy hush. My husband recounted an inspiring Bible story while I illustrated it. Bible stories translate well in any culture, especially in the Third World. Our interpreter threw himself into the role, and even though I was facing my chalkboard, I knew our audience was spellbound, hanging on every word. When I'd finished my sketching, I looked around. The sullenness had disappeared, replaced almost imperceptibly by something else. Was it a fragile interest peeping through that empty dwelling place of the heart?

A few more songs, then the interpreter concluded our concert with a short prayer, inviting any who wished to know more about Jesus to accept a Cambodian New Testament. The chaplain whispered to us that he felt the prisoners had been listening and weighing carefully everything we said. Then we heard a formal speech of thanks from the prison warden, who ended with a stiff bow as I handed over my sketch.

The Word of God had been shared; what more could we do? As the band started up again, we did something usually frowned upon by prison authorities. But it seemed as if the Lord touched our hearts to connect with theirs. Walking among the prisoners, we warmly shook hands with the males and embraced the females. Men with men, and women with women, respecting their customs.

How do I explain what happened next?

The atmosphere changed. An undercurrent was released. A complete transformation unfolded as for the first time, we saw a visible response. Tears welled in the eyes of the prisoners and overflowed. Smiles appeared as shafts of light penetrating the darkness. Women hugged us in return. Men relaxed taut muscles.

What had cut through those strongholds of unbelief and despair, breaking down the mighty barricades of self-preservation?

Why, the power of God alone, through the application of a seemingly small thing: touch. We had touched them, the untouchable. As ambassadors of the living Lord, we had identified with them as individuals, in turn releasing a sudden surge of hope that maybe God could too. Hadn't Jesus identified with them by suffering humiliation at the hands of men who had no mercy? And wasn't he punished for their sins, even though he was innocent? We believe hope was born that day. Hope that things could change.

God had used us to display the power of compassion. The power of touch. The power to set the captives free from the prisons of their souls.

—*Rita S. Galieh*

Gambler or Believer?

If ever I had to put my faith to work, Christmas 2002 was the ultimate test. Little did I know that my annual trip from California to Virginia to spend the holiday season with my mother would be like none other. It began as usual with planning and packing for my trip. On December 22, I arrived in Richmond happy to see my family but feeling a little under the weather.

During the next few days, my mother and I enjoyed Christmas together, but she became concerned that I was suffering from more than just an upset stomach. She thought it might be a recurrence of my colitis, which I had been diagnosed with in 1995. By December 27, I called my physician in Los Angeles and told him about my symptoms. He suggested that I take Imodium A-D, and he phoned in a prescription for me. Unfortunately, my condition continued to deteriorate, so I called my doctor again.

This time he told me that I should see a doctor in Richmond if my condition did not improve.

A few days later, my mother took me to an urgent care facility. Despite our questions about my colitis, the doctor there diagnosed me with a stomach virus and gave me a prescription for stomach cramps. But he did suggest that if I was not better by the next day, I should return for further testing.

The next morning I was worse. My mom and I returned to the facility and saw a different doctor. He immediately knew that I was in trouble and called my doctor in Los Angeles. After a phone consultation, they concluded that I needed to go to the ER to be seen right away.

I arrived at the ER barely able to walk, with a fever of 102. Three hours after I was examined, the ER physician came back to tell us that I had a very serious condition called mega toxic colon. Later that night a specialist arrived. He said, "You are very sick and will die tonight if you don't have your colon removed immediately."

I tried to wrap my mind around what this man, a stranger, had just said. I reached for my mother, who looked exactly the way I felt. The only words that I could get out were, "Mommy, why is he saying this? I must be dreaming."

Realizing how unprepared we were to hear such devastating news, the doctor added, "I know this is scary, but this is your only chance to live."

The specialist continued explaining the procedure and how I would have to have a colostomy bag. My mother was asking about getting a second opinion. I felt as if I were no longer a part of the conversation. Suddenly, it was as if I had been lifted outside of myself and was a spectator of this horrible situation. Then, slowly, I began to feel the desperation disappear and a calm enfold me. When I pulled myself back to the conversation, I firmly stated, "I'm not having the surgery. I know this is not how God wants me to live my life."

The doctor stared at me in disbelief. "What do you mean you're not having the surgery?"

I looked at my mother and repeated my decision. "I'm not having the surgery."

The specialist seemed irritated. "Do you realize that you won't survive the night without the surgery?"

"I don't believe that," I said.

Now impatient and defensive, he added, "I had a patient here a few weeks ago with the same condition, but not nearly as sick as you. She died two hours after she arrived in the ER. You have to have this surgery, or you may not live through the next few hours."

"I'm sorry that happened to the other patient," I said, "but I do not believe that will happen to me. I'm going to stand on my faith in God."

The specialist looked at me like I was crazy. He smirked. "You'll need more than faith to get through this."

"I don't believe I will."

Despite my protests, we were transported to another facility for the surgery. The surgeon introduced himself to my family and me. He sat down beside my bed and began, "You are one sick girl." He told me about the surgery and what the procedure would entail. He explained that I would have to wear a colostomy bag and that in a couple of years reconstructive surgery might be an option. I couldn't believe that I was hearing any of this. I just wanted him to stop. Then he called in his surgery team and introduced them to us. He explained how long the surgery would take and ended by saying, "We need to get started right away."

"I'm not having the surgery," I told him.

In total disbelief he said, "You can't be serious."

I said again, "I'm not having the surgery."

So he tried a new tactic. He showed us what a normal colon looks like, then he showed us what my colon looked like. My colon was more than three times the size of a normal colon, and it was stretched more than humanly possible. Any moment my colon could tear, and I would probably die immediately. He said it was impossible to recover from this condition—he had never seen it happen.

But I continued to tell him that I didn't want the surgery.

He got right up next to my face. "What are you, a gambler? Why would you want to gamble with your life?" He told me that I was playing Russian roulette with my life, and I would probably lose. Then he turned to my mother and asked her why she would gamble with her child's life. He said I would probably not make it through the night. "You all look like intelligent people," he said. "Why are you making such a horrible decision?"

My mother said, "This is her decision, and I stand with her." That was probably one of the hardest choices my mother ever made. I'm her baby girl, her only child. The surgeon could not understand how she would stand by and allow her child to risk her life, but I knew she did it because of her faith in God.

Finally, the surgeon said, "Are you sure you want to take this gamble?"

"I don't believe that I am gambling," I said. "I'm standing on my faith in Jesus."

He sent his surgery team home and sat down beside me. "I have never met anyone like you before." But he said that if I wanted to take the gamble, he would do his best to help me win.

After I spent the night in intensive care, a nurse took me down to get an x-ray. The specialist who had seen me the night before entered. "I see you made it through the night."

"I'm still here," I said.

He said the x-ray showed little improvement in the size of my colon, but it was not any larger. My mother and I were thankful for that, but the doctor still held out little hope.

After another x-ray that night, the surgeon walked up to me, smiling. "You must be something special—truly a miracle!"

My colon had shrunk to half the size it had been less than twenty-four hours earlier. I was elated! I could hardly wait to tell my mom and my other family members.

When I saw my mother, tears of joy began falling down my face. I smiled and gave her the thumbs up. She broke down, and everyone was crying tears of joy. Even the nurse was so moved that she began to cry and hug me and my family.

Each day after that, God continued to shrink my colon to its normal size. My fever broke. I was taken out of ICU and off the monitors. I was given liquids and then slowly put back on solid foods.

It was amazing how my story spread through the hospital. Nurses came by from other wards saying, "You're the girl from L.A. who was so sick."

Everyone seemed moved by my miraculous healing. Even the surgeon came to me and told me how my faith had inspired him. But the specialist had a hard time accepting my stand on faith. He continued to give me pamphlets on the colon procedure and reconstructive surgery, which I tossed in the trash as soon as he left the room. He reminded me I would need a colonoscopy when I returned to L.A., and that test may still reveal bad news.

After I was released from the hospital, I remained at my mom's house to recover and build up my strength. I was weak, I had lost seventeen pounds, and nothing felt familiar. I was taking large doses of steroids that left me feeling dazed, and I rarely slept.

So I continued to pray, read the Bible, and ask the Lord to make me feel like myself again. One day when I was feeling down and calling on the Lord, he reminded me of what he had already done for me and that I needed to be patient because he hadn't gone anywhere. It was a slow process, but eventually I regained most of my strength and some of my appetite.

On January 20, I arrived in Los Angeles feeling stronger. At my appointment with my physician, the nurse broke into tears when I told her what had happened to me. We were both praising God and giving thanks to Him. My doctor was equally amazed. "I guess they thought you were crazy to turn down the surgery."

"Yes, they did," I replied.

Three weeks later, I had a colonoscopy that miraculously showed no damage to my colon, no cancer, and only a touch of colitis. My doctor concluded that I was in great shape and only needed to continue with my medication and annual checkups.

So, am I a gambler? No—never a gambler, but always a believer.

—*Sharon Dolores Thaniel*

Joy in a Jelly Jar

We'd recently sold a nice house to purchase a smaller home with a smaller mortgage payment, but even so, a strict budget was an absolute necessity. Although at times it was a challenge to live within our means, we had a roof over our heads, game meat in the freezer, and an abundance of easy-to-grow vegetables.

Whenever I went to the market for groceries, I took only the shopping list, that week's food allowance in cash, and my trusty red clicker counter. If I took the checkbook, I was tempted to splurge because we had automatic overdraft protection for our bank account, but paying in cash forced me to purchase only the staples. Simple, but it worked.

Following a list is easy enough, but I sometimes allowed unnecessary extras to jump into my cart. Eventually I learned to ask myself before I reached for an item, "Is this necessary for good nutrition, proper hygiene, or health?" Bypassing extras became somewhat easier under that kind of scrutiny.

One particular shopping trip, I breezed through the store, easily sticking to my budgeted list. My son was content in the baby seat, waving at other shoppers and occasionally grabbing at the brightly colored objects we passed. All was going well until I reached the jelly aisle. The endless varieties looked delicious, and my mouth watered over Concord grape, strawberry, raspberry, and plum. I started thinking of a good old PB and J. I could almost taste the thick layer of peanut butter sandwiched between generous slabs of my fresh homemade bread, all slathered with fruity jelly. It was so appealing, I was salivating right there in the supermarket. The cool jar of jelly felt good in my hand as I put it into the cart. I hesitated. Was jelly really necessary or just a luxury? I sighed and reluctantly put the jelly back on the shelf. I took a sip from my ever-present water bottle, trying to wash away the taste of my imagined peanut butter and jelly sandwich.

By the time I finished rounding up the rest of the items on my grocery list, my clicker counter announced a sum below the amount of cash in my purse. I could get one jar of jelly after all! Woo-hoo! I zipped the cart back to the condiments aisle, my son laughing at the sudden change of direction. After much deliberation, I chose a jar of cherry jelly and scurried to the checkout. To my chagrin, the clerk rang up a total that exceeded my expected tally. Confused and embarrassed by my error, I reduced my purchase by several items. The jelly had to go back after all.

I drove home feeling depressed, disappointed, and deprived. Living within our means was far more difficult in real life than it had been on paper, but today I had to trust that the prayerful decisions we'd made regarding our family priorities and finances were more important in the long run than me having the immediate gratification of a peanut butter and jelly sandwich. In my sulking mood, I even had trouble being grateful that we were in good health and had a steady income. But when I caught myself being rude to other drivers, I knew I had to do something proactive to reverse the direction of my thoughts.

In a valiant attempt to regain an attitude of gratitude, right there at a stoplight I started a mental tabulation of my blessings. I worked my way down a list that lengthened by the moment: I had a good husband who had solid employment, and I had the joy-of-my-life toddler chattering happily in the back seat. I was healthy and had a wonderful extended family, etc., etc. By the time I pulled into our driveway, I decided the want of a silly little jar of jelly couldn't overshadow all those blessings. I concentrated on putting the groceries away. What *was* I pouting about?

A knock at the door interrupted my tasks in the pantry. When I went to answer it, I was greeted by my friend Anne's smiling face. I reached out to hug her, but a bulky sack filled her arms.

"I wondered if you could use these," she said. "It's just too much. My family will never finish all this." She held the heavy grocery bag out to give me a peek inside.

Jelly! It was full of jelly! Incredulous, I told Anne about my emotional struggle in the supermarket just an hour ago and about coming home empty-handed. She nodded, relating her sudden strong urge to bring the jelly over to me *now*, not later in the week when we'd see each other anyway. We giggled, deciding that this was not merely a coincidence but another one of those wonderful "God-incidents." We exchanged a warm hug, and I returned to putting my groceries away. From the bag containing Anne's generous gift I lifted out one jar after another—jars full of homemade jellies and jams, in all kinds of wonderful flavors—from fresh fruits grown right in Anne's yard!

At that moment I felt God smiling at me, and I folded another blessing into my already full heart.

—*Maryjo Faith Morgan*

The Missing Jewel

School was over, and the halls were crowded with rushing children hurrying to their buses or carpools. I was picking up my two daughters. I searched the busy crowd of children with their assortment of backpacks and gym bags, looking for them. Then I happened to glance down at my left hand and saw with a shock that the stone of my engagement ring was gone! I was stunned. Where could it have fallen out?

I had just left work, driven to my children's school, and walked across a parking lot. My heart started thumping in panic as I realized I had no idea when or where the stone had disappeared. It could have come loose from its antique setting anywhere. It might have fallen onto the blacktop of the parking lot or onto the floor of the busy school. I tried retracing my exact steps back to my car. The blacktop shimmered in the sun with glistening specks of gravel. It was hopeless to find such a small object in a large, busy area. Children were chattering on the sidewalk, cars were pulling in and out to pick them up, and the school buses were leaving.

My engagement ring was special not only because my husband had given it to me, but also because it had belonged to his grandmother. The gold setting held a simple white sapphire stone, which I had loved wearing for the past eighteen years. I felt even worse about the loss because our wedding anniversary was in a few days.

I thought back to the day when my husband, Jim, surprised me with the ring. We had just gotten engaged. He was a struggling writer, trying to write full-time and work part-time in a bookstore. I knew he couldn't afford an engagement ring. But it didn't matter to me. I was deeply in love with him.

Then one Sunday afternoon, he handed me a small box.

"What's this?" I exclaimed in surprise.

"Open it," Jim said.

Inside was the lovely ring.

"It was my grandmother's," he said. "My mother wanted you to have it. I never knew my grandmother because she died when my mom was a teenager. She was a redhead, which is where I get my red hair from."

I loved the ring, and having something like that handed down to Jim and then me made it even more special.

I roused myself from my reminiscing. How was I going to tell Jim that I lost his grandmother's stone? How would his mom feel? I suddenly felt sadder for them than for myself.

At the same time, I was somehow at peace. That night over supper I told my family about the missing stone. Even though I felt bad, I reasoned, "Well, I can't take the ring with me to heaven someday. I won't need it there. So I guess it's okay that I don't have it anymore." I was a Christian, and my life's focus was not on possessions. I always tried to keep a heavenly perspective. My husband was surprised that the stone had fallen out of the setting, but he was very understanding.

Since it seemed like the stone would be impossible to find, I didn't even bother to pray about finding it until the next day. I tried to look for it at the library where I work, but the gray-speckled carpet made it very difficult to spot something like a small white stone, which would blend in easily. I asked my coworker to help me look, but she didn't find it either. In our busy public library, there are always a lot of people coming, so someone might easily have trampled it or accidentally thrown it out. I figured the cleaning people had vacuumed it up.

I finally decided to pray about it. My prayer was very simple: "Lord, if there is any way the stone to my ring can be found, I would really like it back." I worked the rest of the day but never found the small white stone. I went home, resigned to the fact that I would never be able to wear my engagement ring again. We didn't have the money to just go out and buy a replacement, either.

The next day when I went to work at the library, there on my desk, a little off to one side, lay a small, white, sparkling stone. It was the white sapphire from my engagement ring!

I was amazed and delighted! How was this possible? I thought that I had lost it in the busy school parking lot, but I had actually lost it at work. I have no idea who found my stone or put it on my desk. My coworker had no idea either. To me, it was like an angel put it there. Even if it was some unknowing child who picked the "pretty" up off the floor, it was still a miracle to see it appear on my desk. God answered my simple prayer, but he had waited until I asked.

I lost the stone on Tuesday afternoon. The Lord gave it back to me Thursday morning. Does God answer "impossible" prayers? He certainly does! Does God answer prayers about little things? Yes, definitely.

I am convinced that if we don't ask, we won't receive things from God. There are many good things that the Lord wants us to have but we hesitate to "bother" Him. Yet in the Old Testament, God urged Solomon to ask for whatever he wanted.

Solomon asked for an understanding heart. The Lord gave it to him and much, much more.

We have the freedom to ask God for anything if we have a humble heart and realize that he will give us what is best for us. Every time I look at my hand, I am reminded of God's love for me, because he answered my simple prayer. The real jewel I received was the knowledge that we can pray about anything and that God will answer us.

—*Janet M. Bair*

Surviving the Oklahoma City Bombing

I had a specific goal to accomplish and not much time to complete it. I needed to finish an important presentation for my work at the Water Resource Building, which sat directly next to the Murrah Building. Arriving at work early on the morning of April 19, 1995, I noticed it was pretty quiet in downtown Oklahoma City at 7:00 A.M. "Perfect," I thought. Nothing was going to break my concentration.

When I walked into the office, I found our college intern, Trudy, rarin' to go. She was a single mom, a Christian, and had a real passion for her work. She often arrived at the office before me. In fact, it had almost become a game for the two of us to see who could get there first. I liked Trudy, but this morning I couldn't afford to be sidetracked by her friendly chitchat. After a quick "Good morning," I got pretty short with her, letting her know I had a lot of hard work to do and no time to visit. The look on her face told me she was hurt. I felt a twinge of guilt, but I had maps to finish.

After about an hour and a half, I had accomplished a big portion of my work, sending thirteen maps to the color printer upstairs. I had already decided not to check on them until I was completely finished. Then something made me change my mind. I walked past Trudy and Mike, another of my coworkers, who were busy at their desks, to go upstairs.

Just as I walked into the third-floor printing room, the loudest bang I've ever heard literally lifted the building. I saw sky above me before the roof came crashing back down. Every window in front of me was shattered into a million pieces, and all the ceiling tiles and wiring came thundering down around my head as I raised my arms to protect myself.

"What in the world?" was all I could say. When my hearing came back, I heard two women running to me. Covered in blood and dust, they frantically attached themselves to my arms. I asked if they were okay, then we groped our way to the hall. To the right was an emergency exit, but the roof had caved in and jammed the doorframe. There was no way to open it.

The women started toward the stairs in the center of the building, and though they were just a few steps in front of me, they literally disappeared into the thick dust. Worried about what might be in the center of the building, I turned back to the first exit. I strained to pull open the door, using more force than I'd known I had. Miraculously, it opened just enough so a person could duck through. I called out for the two women, and they reappeared with more coworkers. We headed out into the alley, where a horrible chemical smell overcame us. Everyone was pouring out of the buildings all around, crying, moaning, and screaming. I immediately tried to get a head count. It was difficult, because everyone was in shock and couldn't think clearly.

When I realized Mike and Trudy were unaccounted for, I ran back to my floor to search for them. Heading down the hall, I was forced to stop. I believe I was about twenty feet from our office, but everything looked different. There was a huge pile of twisted metal, electrical wire, and large chunks of the building where our work area should have been. I called out for Trudy and Mike several times but received no answer. I went back outside, hoping they had gone out the back door while I was going out the front. I searched everywhere from groups of workers gathered on the curb to the corner they were calling "triage." The officials were already cordoning off the area. I was worried. No one had seen Mike or Trudy. I found myself wandering between three areas, checking for my friends. In front of me, I saw the biggest fireman I'd ever seen.

"He's so strong, he'll be able to help me," I thought. Reaching up to put my hand on his solid muscular shoulder, I asked him if he could help me find my friends. He turned to look at me, and I saw the same shock that everyone else wore on their faces. He sadly shook his head. Then I knew that only God could help us through this.

A stranger with a cell phone dialed my wife's number for me. She didn't answer, so I left a message. Just as I said, "I'm okay," into the phone, the weight of the world seemed to hit me. I couldn't believe the feeling. I was okay but not okay. Handing back the phone, I became disoriented and confused. I continued to wander until a coworker directed me to a group from our office where we just stood in disbelief for about thirty minutes. Then my wife walked right up to our corner, holding our thirteen-month-old daughter. The emotion poured out of me as I sobbed on her shoulder. I had never been happier yet hurting so badly at the same time.

I found out Mike was injured but alive. It took two weeks to find out Trudy had been killed in our office. I felt so guilty for surviving when she had died. If only I would have known it was my last time to see her, I would have treated her with more love and respect. I wondered why God had left me here. Somehow I knew I had something really important to do. I just wished it were spelled out clearly for me.

I watched the TV coverage for a month, trying to make sense of such horror. The television accounts seemed so trivial compared to the real thing. My world had been shaken so badly; I felt so lost.

Officials planned a national memorial service and asked all the survivors to come. President Bill Clinton and many other important people spoke, but nothing seemed to make me feel better. Then Billy Graham got up and spoke God's Word in a simple, reassuring way that spoke right to me. A deep peace washed over me—the same peace I had had as a child when I went down to the altar at a Billy Graham crusade to dedicate my life to the Lord. I knew everything would be okay. God was still God. I will always remember Trudy and many of my other friends who died. Perhaps one of the most important reasons God left me here is to treat every person I talk to with love and respect. Each encounter with every person is holy, for it could be the last chance I ever get to talk to them.

—*Brad Nesom as told to Eva Juliuson*

Smarts Aren't Enough

It was Saturday night, and as usual Elsa invited us to her home for dinner. She was an elderly lady of German descent who lived alone and enjoyed entertaining. We always looked forward to her famous German cooking, which we had enjoyed so many times. When Elsa's husband was alive, they had always entertained on Saturday nights, and it seems she just couldn't give up the habit. Elsa had been a teenager in Berlin during World War II. At one point she had gone to prison for listening to American radio broadcasts, and then one of the American soldiers who had liberated her from prison became her husband! I loved to listen to her after-dinner stories.

We were ministering in a new church in Florida in a large senior community. Seniors were moving into that area by the hundreds, so churches were needed. Elsa had recently joined our little congregation. She had been sharing her faith with some of her neighbors, and unknown to us, she had invited one of those couples to join us that evening.

Walter and Alicia had known Elsa for some time. Both had lost their mates before they met and entered into this second union. Walter was ninety-two and in his working days had been the "lawyer's lawyer." He was a stately man with white hair and a vocabulary that would put *Webster's Dictionary* to shame. In his argyle vest and bow tie, he seemed to be one of the last of a bygone era. His wife, Alicia, was a very proper lady originally from England who deferred to her husband in every way. She was many years younger, but it seemed her years had worn on her, making her look closer to Walter's age.

It was apparent that Walter wanted everyone to realize how important he had been before he retired. He dazzled us with his vast treasure of words. He had written books on law and taught in law schools in California. There was no doubt that he was a powerful orator even at his present age; he had all the answers, no matter the discussion, and talked about himself all through dinner so that no one else could get a word into the conversation.

After dinner our hostess invited us to proceed to the living-room sofa. Anxious for a break in Walter's monologue, I got up and headed in that direction. Just behind me followed Walter. Ernie, my husband, had not realized that Walter's wife, Alicia, had waited all evening to get to speak with him concerning her spiritual life. So she stayed behind at the table, taking a quick opportunity to get away from her husband and engage Ernie with her questions. I thought, "Oh, no, Lord, you're giving me the job of occupying Walter so that this lady can receive spiritual guidance. Oh well, if that's my divine appointment, I'll do it," I prayed with a resigned sigh.

Walter and I ended up in the living room alone. I kept hoping the others would soon make their way in to join us and spare me from being the captive audience. I tried to make some small talk, but each comment ended with Walter setting off his vast verbiage like a fireworks display, leaving me sitting in awe and wonder at all the syllables spewing forth from his lips. All at once he stopped in the middle of one such display and said, "Linda, I'd like to ask you a question."

"Oh, no," I thought, "He's going to test my word power and make determinations about my IQ."

He went on. "I am 92 years old and realize that sometime soon my life will end. In your opinion, will I go to heaven?"

I'm sure my jaw dropped at such an open door. So many times I've prayed, "Lord, give me a soul to lead to you," and now despite my anxious boredom, this elderly gentleman was asking for the way to spend eternity in the presence of God. I immediately perked up, and my soul-winning classes came to mind. I said, "Walter, it all hinges on your answer to this question: If you met God at heaven's gate tonight and he asked you why he should let you into his heaven, what would you answer?"

Walter went into some ethereal discussion about how he had been a good person and had given money to good causes. The oral discourse went on and on until suddenly he stopped and said, "Did I give the right answer?"

I said, "Walter, the only reason God will allow you into his heaven is if you've repented of sin and accepted his Son, Jesus, as Savior and Lord of your life. Jesus said, 'No man cometh to the Father, but by me.' Has there been a time in your life when you've repented of your sin and asked Jesus to come live within and through you?"

Another round of endless suppositions followed, so I put my hand on his arm and said, "Walter, you know, you're right; you may not have long to live. You can't leave tonight without knowing for sure that you're going to heaven. Another lawyer went to Jesus one night and said, 'Master, what must I do to be saved?' And Jesus gave him this answer: 'Except a man is born again, he cannot see the Kingdom of heaven' (John 3:3. KJV). Would you like that assurance?"

He mutely nodded his head yes.

I immediately began to lead Walter in a prayer of repentance, inviting Jesus Christ into his life. I had to do some repenting, too, for not looking for an opportunity to share my faith. I had gone to dinner expecting my own needs to be met. I had mentally pushed Walter away because of his personality. I hadn't seen him with the eyes of love. I wonder how many other opportunities I'd missed. This experience was a brush with reality. There are many people who are seeking the way into the presence of God; if I get caught up in my own needs and concerns, I won't see those around me who are in greater need.

After Walter and I prayed, the other dinner guests entered the room. We announced to them that Walter knew he was on his way to heaven. We all rejoiced together. A short time later, we gave our thanks to our hostess and left. The next day Elsa called and told me that Walter, full of joy, had phoned her and said that Mrs. Henson was the smartest woman he had ever met!

—*Linda R. Henson*

He Hears and Answers

I picked up the phone to find my friend, Joy Pack, calling from her hospital bed at home. "Evelyn, you and Ted are going to Sea World in Ohio for a couple of days, because I know you need a vacation!"

I didn't feel much like laughing, but I managed a chuckle as I asked how a trip to Sea World was possible?

"Let me tell you how the Lord worked it out," she explained.

Joy. It means "to experience great pleasure and delight, to rejoice with gladness, to be happy beyond measure." With that definition in mind, our friends Ethel and Joe had given their baby girl born with spina bifida that name. Being paralyzed from the waist down hadn't stopped Joy as a toddler. Her ready smile and a toss of her thick black hair greeted all who came to visit. Her dad would strap her onto a skateboard, and with her little arms flying, she maneuvered through the whole house with abandon.

Later on as she grew, she was confined to a wheelchair with a heavy brace holding her body upright. But in spite of all that, she became the epitome of her name—*Joy*.

So, Joy proceeded to explain to me how our trip to Sea World came about. She was a regular listener of WJYP, a radio station featuring Christian music and commentary. A few days earlier, WJYP was offering two free tickets to Sea World to the first caller who could identify a certain set of songs. Joy told her mother, "Ted and Evelyn are deeply grieved and exhausted from losing two parents in such a short time, so I have asked the Lord to let me win those tickets, just for them." Joy listened carefully to the melodies, copying the names of the songs on a piece of paper, and she dialed WJYP at the first opportunity. She was the first one to get the songs right!

"Go pick up your tickets at WJYP," Joy told me on the phone. "I won them just for you two, so you could get out of town for a few days of rest. You need a vacation."

Deeply touched by her efforts, Ted and I accepted Joy's offer of the two tickets to Sea World. That her prayers on our behalf had been answered was with us every moment during the three carefree days we spent watching aquatic shows and petting dolphins. We returned from the vacation refreshed, our sadness and depression lifted. So Joy could always remember the kindness she showed us, we brought her a darling white baby seal back to add to her large stuffed-animal collection.

Nurtured by her parents' constant care, Joy attended public schools all the way through high school, where she became a loyal and faithful fan of her football team. She rarely missed a game during her four years at Capital High, and the team eagerly awaited the arrival of the petite young girl who boisterously cheered them on from her wheelchair nearby.

When Joy was a senior and plans for the prom were completed, Ethel confided to a few friends that her daughter's prayers had begun to include a special plea. Joy was asking the Lord to let her attend prom with a date, "just like all the other girls," Ethel told us. This brought us all great pain, because none of us thought that her prayer would be answered. Joy had never had a date, nor a boyfriend, and how could she join in the activities, even if she were to attend? Those of us who knew about Joy's desire were heart-broken to hear that this sweet girl trusted the Lord for the impossible. I, who had no faith at all that Joy's prayers would be answered, earnestly sought the Lord, asking him to comfort Joy when she had to face the bitter disappointment of unanswered prayer.

Then out of the blue Joy's father got a phone call. It was a boy on the high school football team—and he had a request: "May I take your daughter to the prom?" he asked. He explained that he knew Joy was an avid fan who supported the team, win or lose, and had often talked to her because she parked her wheelchair near the team's bench during the games. "I admire your daughter," the young man said, "and it would be an honor to escort her to the prom."

Of course, Joe said yes. Joy had never once doubted that God would hear and answer her prayers. I bawled my eyes out at the news. "O ye of little faith," I thought.

Ethel and Joy shopped for a special gown that would fit around Joy's chair. They found the perfect one: white with lots of red trim and a long, full skirt. Joe put special decorations all over her chair, and Joy went to the prom with a date, just like all the other girls. Everyone watched, teary-eyed, as her football team hero pushed her wheelchair onto the floor to dance. It was the highlight of her years at Capital High, and it was a lesson to me to be more trusting in sincerely offered prayers.

On the day Joy got her diploma, there was not a dry eye at Capital High School, including those of her proud parents. It had been a struggle for her, getting that diploma, but she had done it. The entire student body stood applauding as Joy wheeled across the stage to receive it.

Though Joy was ill and on oxygen for most of the rest of her life, she stayed busy doing volunteer work for several charities. She also helped in her church office and with the AWANA (Approved Workmen Are Not Ashamed, from 2 Timothy 2:15) program for young children, all the while keeping an eye on her friends so she could be an encouragement when needed.

Joy had served her parents, her friends, and her Lord for twenty-nine years when she was called away from us. As I write this, the little white seal pup we bought for her at Sea World now looks down on me from its perch in my home. You see, Joy knew she was going to her real home, so she asked her mom to see that Ted and I got the seal back as a parting gift from her. Every time I glance its way I am reminded of our friend Joy who had great and unfailing faith. When she asked the Lord for a date to the prom, she knew something I didn't—that our heavenly Father loves us and listens to all our prayers—even those of physically challenged little girls—and he answers.

—*Evelyn Rhodes Smith*

 Woodpecker King

Amovement in the trees at the edge of my vision suddenly caught my eye. "What was that?" I wondered as I whipped my head around. I stared intently through the maze of brown branches bordering our yard, feeling hope well up inside of me. There—I saw it again. "Yes!" I cried aloud. The size of the bird and its brilliant red crest told me that the pileated woodpecker had come to our yard for his breakfast.

A magnificent specimen of some twelve to fifteen inches in length, this bird is beautiful even in flight. Its white underpinning contrasts sharply with its black body so that it seems to wave at me momentarily before it lands on another tree. But it's that incredible red headdress above its black-and-white-striped face that crowns this bird as king of the woodpecker world in this part of Ohio.

I've known for some time that a pileated woodpecker frequented our area. Last spring he all but destroyed an ailing tree in our front yard in his eagerness to eat the insects that lived and multiplied beneath the bark. The tree now sports a hollowed out-cavity nearly eight feet in length after the woodpecker's drilling made the tree's true condition known to us, its unsuspecting property owners. So badly did he tear up the tree trunk that my husband no longer welcomes his presence on our property, fearing that he'll do the same to the rest of the timber in the yard.

But I find him impossible to resist. I still gasp in wonder each time he makes an appearance, my gaze riveted on him until he flies away. Moving from one tree to the next, he works his way slowly through the yard until he finally flies out of my field of view. I'm always slightly amazed each time that I just happened to be in the right place at the right time to catch a peek at him. Then I think about that moment on and off during the rest of the day.

The same thing happens when the King of Kings suddenly blesses my morning devotional time with his presence. It happens frequently that I'll be sitting at the table, a cup of coffee in hand, concentrating on things of the Lord, when suddenly in my spiritual vision I catch just a glimpse of movement in the supernatural realm. In the blink of an eye, an idea pops into my mind and just as quickly flies away. I stare intently in that direction, hoping to get a glimpse of it once more. Slowly it seems to head my way, growing in size and clarity as it moves ever nearer my conscious understanding. Like the woodpecker, who teases me by vanishing behind the backside of trees only to pop his head out on one side or the other again moments later, the spiritual insight also seems to dart in and out of my awareness until it eventually pops fully into view and I gasp in wonder at the understanding of the elusive concept. Gratitude and wonder at what God has to say follow quickly on the heels of comprehension. I carry the memory of the moment for the rest of the day, applying it as a balm to remedy hurtful situations I may find myself in later.

I've known for a long time that God lives in my world, surrounding me at all times with his presence. But, oh, the wonder of being at just the right spiritual place to actually catch a glimpse of him as he moves throughout my life, and to spend a little time looking more closely into what he's doing in my life and heart!

Sometimes his work seems painfully destructive—a tearing apart of the covering I've placed over secret sins and attitudes, hiding their presence from the watching world, but not from its Creator. He knows what lies beneath the outer covering, and he pecks away at it until he exposes the worms that eat at my spiritual life. He cleans me out of that which would eventually lead to my death. This tendency of his sometimes makes him an unwelcome visitor and causes some Christians to place fences around areas that they're not willing to give him access to. But others of us find him simply irresistible. The beauty of his nature and the wonder of what he has to say force me to keep my eyes locked on his visage for as long as he chooses to be visible to me that day. But it's his shed red blood, poured out at the cross that first catches my attention and then crowns him as King in my life and my heart.

—*Elaine L. Bridge*

He Was There
All Along

I didn't go to our regular church that Sunday morning because my brother, who is a preacher, was in town preaching at a different church, and I had decided to go hear him instead. It was a busy morning, with my getting ready to go to church across town, and my husband, Michael, and our three girls getting ready to go to our regular church.

As usual, Michael hobbled along slowly through the Sunday morning routine. It had been over a year since his back surgery, but Michael was still in pain, and it was only getting worse. Just looking at him made me cringe inside. I was *so* tired of seeing him in constant, excruciating pain.

I kept asking God, "Why? Why must he suffer so much? Are you even there? Do you even care?" I told myself over and over again that, yes, God was with us, and he had his reasons for putting us through this trial. But these days, did I really believe it? After a year past with no relief from Michael's pain, I was truly beginning to doubt. It wasn't like me to doubt God, but it just didn't feel like he knew our situation at all, or at least didn't care about it. It felt like he'd forgotten all about us.

Soon my mom picked me up for church, and we went off to hear my brother preach. I gave Michael a hug and kiss good-bye, and out the door I went, hoping he would be able to handle taking all three girls to church, considering the pain he was in.

Throughout the church service that I sat through, I continued to wonder where God was. I tried to listen to my brother's message, but I'd grown tired, almost too tired to really hear or care. I was tired of the burden of caring for the girls falling on my shoulders; tired of seeing Michael lie on the bed, suffering; tired of him not even being able to work because of the constant pain; tired of his neurosurgeon telling us that there was nothing more that he could do for him. Tired. I was just plain tired. Where was God? Did he know that Michael was in constant pain?

At the end of the church service I was attending, Michael and the girls were there to pick me up. Michael seemed to be doing okay for the moment, so that was a good thing.

"How was church today?" I asked him as I climbed in and sat down.

"It was great." He smiled. I could see that he had something to tell me.

"What? Did something happen?" I asked. Of course, now I was just dying to find out what I'd missed out on at our regular church, wishing I'd gone with them instead.

"Yeah, something really cool happened."

"Did you go up for prayer?" I asked. Michael went up for prayer often, in the hopes of finding healing for his back pain—healing that never came. And that was why I was so certain the Lord had forgotten us.

"No," Michael said. "I just didn't feel like going up for prayer today. I thought about it, but I made the decision to stay back."

"So," I asked with eyes wide, "what happened, then?"

"Well," he said, "while other people were going up for prayer, I just stayed back to sing the worship songs. Someone I'd never spoken to before came up to me." Michael was looking back and forth between me and the road as he continued to drive. "He came up and told me something that pretty much blew me away."

"What?" I clenched my hands together. The suspense was killing me!

"He said, 'I don't know why, but I've been standing back there behind you, and I have the strongest feeling from the Lord that I'm to come over to you, lay my hands on your back, and pray for it.'" Michael smiled. "The man went on to ask me, 'Do you have back problems?'"

My heart melted when I heard those words. The Lord really did know about Michael's back pain, and he cared about it enough to send someone over to pray for him—maybe even with miraculous results, or so I hoped.

Michael went on. "I laughed and said, 'Do I have back problems?' And I proceeded to tell him my entire story. After that, he laid his hands on my back and prayed for me."

"Does your back feel better?" I asked, hope welling up inside my heart.

"Well, actually, my back still feels the same. But it was the hugest confirmation to me that the Lord is with me, and he knows exactly what's going on."

It might not have been the miracle I was hoping for, but it was reminder I needed. Here I'd felt as if the Lord had left us—that he didn't even know my husband was suffering from back pain. Instead, God had moved the heart of a stranger, someone who knew nothing about Michael's back problem, and used him to pray for Michael's back. It was now obvious to me that the Lord had not left us—he was with us, and he'd never left us to begin with. He wanted prayer for Michael's back to be lifted up to him, and he moved in another person to make it happen.

It wasn't but a month later when a situation transpired that allowed Michael to go and get a second opinion about his back from a different neurosurgeon. This neurosurgeon found Michael's problem, the source of his pain. He said that a second surgery could fix Michael and make his pain go away—once and for all.

The Lord didn't miraculously heal Michael, but he showed himself to us in an unbelievable, amazing way. It made me realize that I should never doubt him. I should never, even for a second, think that he's forgotten us or doesn't know what's going on in our lives. He's not like us; he's omnipotent—he sees all and he knows all, down to the tiniest details.

For all I know, it was the prayer from that stranger in church that opened the doors for us to get the second opinion, which gave us the answers we'd been praying for all along.

—Karin A. Lovold

The Master's Voice

"Turn around now." That's what the still small voice in my head kept saying. I had passed by this particular Tae Kwon Do academy dozens of times, each time feeling the urge to stop and register my children for classes. For several weeks, I had resisted the internal nudge, remembering the conversation I'd had with my husband, reasoning with myself—we can't afford it, and there are several schools much closer to home than this one. What was it about this place, that it seemed God was leading me there?

Some months before I ever felt this leading, I had read an article in *Attention!* magazine about how Tae Kwon Do was beneficial to children with ADHD. Since both of my children have learning disabilities, I knew that these martial arts classes might have a very positive effect. My husband and I discussed it, and although he agreed that it could very well enhance their lives, we would have to wait until October, because we did not have room in the budget right now.

Now it was a Tuesday in June. I had just driven past the academy. "*Turn around now!*"

The voice was very strong this time. Feeling compelled to obey, I turned my minivan around and went back to the academy. As I parked my car, I noticed that the Korean flag and the American flag were prominently displayed in the front window. I walked into the school and noticed a very distinguished man in the office, which was adjacent to the training floor. He spotted me in the doorway and motioned me over to speak with him. I thought from his graying hair that he was about fifty years old. He spoke English with a heavy Korean accent. He took care to enunciate, but it still took concentration on my part to understand his words. Above the doorway to his office hung a sign that read "Tae Kwon Do Master." Again I wondered why God wanted us *here*.

The master described the many benefits that his classes had for children with learning disabilities. He was a disciplined man who obviously had spent much of his life in training. He was a different kind of master. As I looked around his office, I saw a framed university degree touting a master's degree in education. I was impressed by my first meeting with this master. Because of a summer enrollment special, I decided to sign up my children for summer classes, despite our previous decision to wait until fall. I was thrilled that the lessons could now fit into our budget. Maybe, I thought, this was the reason God had sent me here today.

To get things started, I had many disclosures to read and various forms to fill out. As I handed them back to the master, he immediately noticed that my husband was an attorney with the local utility company. He asked me several questions about what he did for the company, and I explained that he was a tax attorney.

The master began to tell me of the legal troubles he had been having over the last several years with my husband's company. He told me of late fees and penalties, late fees for the penalties, penalties on the late fees, and interest on past due amounts. It sounded like a real headache. He told me that he had spent considerable amounts of money on legal fees fighting this billing error but that his current attorney had not made any progress during the last year. It seems the two of them had been unable to speak with anyone at the utility company to expedite a resolution for this issue. Meanwhile, more and more penalties were being tacked on. He asked if maybe my husband could give him the name of a person that either he or his attorney could talk to, someone in charge.

Before I left his office, I promised to see what my husband could do to help. As soon as the kids and I got settled in the car, I called my husband, Chris, on my cell phone. I explained the Tai Kwon Do master's situation and asked him to see what he could do. My husband said he would try to help, but since he didn't know the person who managed the billing department, he could not make any promises. After all, it is a very large company.

My husband spent the better part of the day talking with various people at the company, from the company operator to the billing clerks to the head of billing. When he called me at that evening, he said, "I did all that I could do. The rest is in God's hands."

The following week when I brought the kids to their Tae Kwon Do class, the master greeted me with great enthusiasm. He began thanking me over and over, explaining that not only was this controversy over, but the utility company was sending him a check for almost $6,000. I was so happy for him, and I was happy that we could help. More importantly, I was excited to be used by God in some small way. I was pleased that I had finally listened to my Master's still small voice telling me to stop at that Tai Kwon Do school.

I couldn't wait to share the news with Chris. When I called him and told him about the master's refund, he said, "Wow, now you know why you were supposed to go there! God wanted us to help him out." That evening when we prayed together, we thanked God for allowing us to be used to help someone.

I had a renewed joy as I took the kids for their Tai Kwon Do lesson the next day. When we walked in, the master called us in to his office. He thanked me again and said that now he needed to do something for me in return. He told me that he wanted to continue teaching my kids—free of charge. He handed me gym bags filled with expensive new uniforms and protective fighting gear for the kids. He then handed me a bill for the classes and equipment. He had written the words "No Charge" across the face of the bill as a receipt.

God's voice telling me to "turn around now" had seemed to defy human logic but now made perfect sense. We could definitely afford lessons that were free of charge!

Often when God speaks to us, we don't understand why he wants us to do what he is telling us. But if we step out in faith, he always rewards us.

—*Pauline Zeilenga*

The Empty Place

Growing up, I was the skinny kid who wore glasses and was the brunt of many jokes. I was the average student who just got by.

I was the kid with the empty place inside.

In my youth, I tried to fill it with athletics. I was an above-average athlete with grand dreams of being a professional baseball player. But when I graduated from high school at 5'8" tall and weighing 135 pounds, my dreams of professional baseball died, and I still had my empty place.

I left home to attend college and found new ways to fill that empty place—parties and alcohol. I was a party animal my freshman year but realized that if I didn't focus more on school, I'd be back home digging ditches or working in a bread factory (a horrible job I once had). I focused my attention on school and graduated with a degree in business. A week after graduating, I married my college sweetheart, and a month later I started an excellent corporate job.

Surely a great marriage and career would fill that empty place.

Within a few years of working in the business world, I realized that I just didn't fit the corporate mold. Even with some outstanding successes and quick promotions, I still felt empty inside. So I quit my management-level job to start my own business. I was convinced that the freedom of owning a business would fill that empty place.

Two years later I was divorced, my business had failed, my car had been repossessed, and I was sitting in a 900 square-foot apartment doing something I had never done before—contemplating suicide. The empty place had grown into a huge, gaping hole that made me ache daily, and I was not sure I could go on. I thought about the various ways I could do it and what they might feel like. Then I considered the effect it would have on my young daughter, my parents, and my friends. Something rose up inside of me that kept me from going forward with my plans to end my life—it was hope.

I had never been a religious person. Oh, I grew up in church, but I turned away from it when I went off to college. I couldn't stand the hypocrisy of organized religion. I believed in God, but not in religion. I know now that it was God who was there with me that awful day and gave me hope.

I didn't end my life that day. Instead, I began looking for a job. I would dress in my only suit and ride the bus to interviews. Soon I secured a job teaching marketing at a technical college, and things were looking up again. I also had a great new relationship with a wonderful woman, and soon we married. Again, I was hoping that this new career and new marriage would fill my empty place.

The job went great, but the marriage was tumultuous at first. I was expecting my wife to fill the empty place, but she was unable to. I turned to my job, but it could not fill that place either. So, once again, I turned to business. I quit my job to start another business. This time the business was very successful and produced something that I had never experienced before—financial freedom and time for recreation. Surely money and free time would fill the void inside of me. But it didn't. I continued to be empty. I cried out for what would fill that place inside me, for what would complete me.

My wife and children started attending church, and after a year of watching the changes in them, I thought that perhaps I was missing something. Maybe church could fill the empty place. I started attending a Sunday evening service, and although it was wonderful, I was still empty and struggling with life.

One Saturday evening we attended a dramatic performance at the church, and at the end they called people forward to receive Jesus as their Lord and Savior. I thought that this might be the answer, so I went forward and went through the motions, repeating the prayer of salvation. But nothing changed in my life. I was still empty and struggling.

A couple years later I attended a Promise Keepers event and stood in the Seattle Kingdome with 52,000 men singing songs about God. I was moved to tears, and my heart broke that day. I stood and wept for the first time since I was a child. Finally, through that brokenness, God began to fill my empty place. Not all at once, but a little at a time.

I came back from Seattle a new person. My wife and friends noticed the difference. I had opened myself to God and was truly a new person.

Although I had been attending church for a couple of years, I had tried my best to blend into the large congregation. This changed after my Promise Keepers experience, as I got involved in men's ministry and started an accountability group with three other guys. Over time I continued to grow in my understanding of the Bible and God. The more I grew, the smaller that empty place got.

A few years later, I felt directed to attend a class at our church, where I met an incredible teacher. In just a few weeks I learned more about myself and my relationship with God than I had in all the previous years of my life combined. The teacher and I became great friends and spent many hours talking about our futures. We met weekly with a group of other men, and all of us went on out-of-town retreats together. It was an amazing feeling to have that many close friends who were all traveling on the same spiritual path.

Out of that group, God birthed a church, pastored by that teacher. My wife and I were part of the founding team, and within six months I felt called into the ministry and became an associate pastor. I used the talents and skills that God had already given me to help the church grow and prosper. As I gave of myself as a servant, the empty place continued to shrink to the point where I rarely even thought about it.

Recently I have been called away from my pastoral position to be a full-time writer. I have loved to write since I was sixteen years old, and now I am doing what I was put on this earth to do. I have a wonderful marriage, five incredible children, and three amazing grandchildren. Life is good, and the empty place is gone. Don't get me wrong, I still have life struggles, but I always know where to go if I start feeling empty.

For years I tried to fill that empty place with activities, alcohol, friends, relationships, business, and success. All along, our loving God was right there guiding me. Even though I didn't recognize or acknowledge him, he was there. I know that it grieved him to see me suffer through all those years, and I'm sure that he was there by my side, patiently waiting for me to open myself to him so he could finally fill my empty place.

It saddens me to see so many people traveling the same road I did. They are empty and trying to fill that empty place with drugs, alcohol, money, sex, relationships, travel, religion of various types, and spiritual paths and beliefs. If they would just realize that there is only one way to fill that void. It is a void we are born with. As a baby, we cry out to our parents to fill the void; as children we cry out to our friends to fill the void; as teenagers we cry out to our peers to fill the void; as adults we cry out to the world to fill the void. Instead, we should be crying out to God to fill that empty place, because it is shaped exactly like him.

—Rod Nichols

In His Hands

"I've been crocheting something special for you," Mom said as we drove along the rural highway one sunny September day. "Remind me to give it to you when we get there."

Ever since Dad had died, she busied herself with crocheting. "It gives me something to do," was her simple explanation when people remarked at all the doilies and edgings she made. She used so much crochet cotton that I finally bought it for her twelve skeins at a time. "Mercy! But I'll never use it all!" was her usual reaction when she'd open a new box. It wouldn't be long, however, until she'd be phoning for more.

"So what have you crocheted this time?" I asked as we left the main highway and turned south along the gravel road. "Oh, you'll see," was all she said.

Mom had been visiting me in the city, and we were driving back to the big old farmhouse she still called home. On either side of the road, combines were gobbling up the last of the prairie wheat crops. When I opened the car window a crack, the familiar smell of grain dust drifted in on the autumn air.

We were now passing through the little village where I'd gone to school. The grain elevator still towered over a scattering of homes and businesses, including the Red and White General Store where I had bought penny candy as a child. Beside it was the small post office where I had waited for love letters from the fellow who became my husband.

A mile west, the old home place came into view. It seemed so withdrawn now, sitting quietly under the tall elm trees that shaded it. I pulled the car to a stop beside the clump of basswoods and opened the trunk to get Mom's suitcase. A bag of groceries stood beside it, and a box of crochet cotton. Mom walked ahead of me along the crumbling cement pathway to unlock the back door of the house.

As she fiddled with the key, I looked across the big front yard where I had spent so many safe and happy hours as a child. Down at the end was the maple that had held my tire swing. My pretend playhouse had stood beside the columbine bush, and I had picked its berries to decorate my mud pies. Hanging from the lowest limb of the elm was a birdhouse, where wrens still nested year after year.

"The house always gets so stuffy when it's been closed up for a few days," Mom said as I entered. "Leave the door open."

She tugged at the pull chain of a light bulb. "Well, the power's still on. I'll just see if the phone's working." Reassured that the utility companies had not failed in her absence, she set about making a fire in the kitchen stove. I watched her light a match and hold it to the crumpled newspaper. Before long a crackling fire chased away the autumn chill. "Would you like a cup of tea before you drive back to the city?" Mom asked.

She took down her Brown Betty teapot from the top of the McClary stove while I went out to pump some fresh water.

"Oh, yes!" she said as we waited for the tea kettle to boil. "Before I forget I must get that piece of crocheting I did for you." Returning from a back room, she began to unroll a large piece of blue tissue paper on the dining room table. "Don't tell me!" she suddenly exclaimed.

"What's wrong?" I asked, hearing the deep disappointment in her voice.

"I put so much work into this, and now look!" She pointed to the tiny puncture marks in the paper. "All that work, and I bet a miserable little mouse ruined it while I was gone!"

She quickly finished unrolling the blue tissue paper. Spread out on it was a large piece of filet crochet, a type that is made up of tiny little squares, some open, some filled in.

"It needs to be framed against a dark background to make it stand out, but can you tell who it is?"

Looking carefully, I could see a picture of Christ, his hands folded in prayer. Above him were the words, "The world is in his hands." Mom never said as much, but I had the feeling she had crocheted the picture not only to acknowledge my Christian faith, but also to convey her own.

I looked at the picture again, trying to imagine the long hours it had taken to make.

As Mom went to the kitchen to steep the tea, I noticed her wipe away a tear with the corner of her bib apron. "I should have known better than to store it away where a mouse might find it."

"I don't see any damage," I said hopefully.

"Look again."

Her hunch was right. Closer inspection revealed several cut threads, right at the tip of Christ's fingers. I think I was just about as disappointed as Mom.

We sat in silence for a while, drinking our tea, when suddenly I had an idea. Her eyes brightened as I shared it with her.

We visited a bit more, and then I said, "I guess I should be going. Thanks for the tea. It sure tastes good made from well water."

"And thank you for the ride home," she said. "And I'll get right busy on that little piece of crocheting."

A few days later the postman delivered a parcel to my door. When I opened it, there was the familiar blue tissue paper protecting the picture of Christ. Pinned to a note in my mother's handwriting was a tiny crocheted cross. "Your eyes would be better than mine to do the rest," was all it said.

That evening, using a needle and white thread, I carefully placed the tiny cross in Christ's hands, stitching so as to mend and cover the broken threads. I was pleased with the results. Not only was the repair almost unnoticeable, the picture now had double the meaning—a reminder of both the great sacrifice Christ made on the cross as well as his intercessory prayers on our behalf. Just as Mom had suggested, I framed the piece of crocheting over a dark background so the image would stand out. She was delighted. Instead of being ruined, her picture had been restored.

Mom has long since passed on, and today when visitors pause to admire the picture she crocheted, they never surmise the damage that was once inflicted by a hungry little mouse. I tell them about it only because it represents that deeper story of how the cross has reconnected the broken threads of my own life. Granted, there are still those little doubts that sometimes nibble away at my faith in God, especially when I view all the damage occurring in the social fabric of our country, but when I look at Mom's picture, I still believe, as she did, that the world is in his hands.

—Alma Barkman

Beyond Frustration

It was a Friday evening at about 5:30, and I had just backed into the pickup truck parked next to the building behind me. I let a few words that Christian ladies shouldn't say slip from my lips as I thought about my missed insurance payment last month. Not to mention, the parking lot I was pulling out of was that of a prospective employer.

My first thought was to leave and not even tell anyone I was the one who did it. But just minutes ago, while making small talk during the job interview, I had mentioned that I always report all my income to the IRS, which gave the interviewer the impression I am an honest person. Needless to say, lying wouldn't work, because I'm not good at it.

Besides, I thought, as I surveyed the damage done, "there's green paint from my car right on the dent, and they're gonna know I was the last person parked here."

After determining that the best thing to do was to fess up, I pictured myself walking back into the office and facing the interviewer and the owner of the company shaking their heads, wrinkling their brows, and pointing at me with extreme disapproval. That imaginary confrontation was enough to convince me to get in my car and drive home—I'd call and leave a message instead.

As I drove out of the parking lot, I was shaking my head vigorously, sending more bad words to heaven along with my other complaints.

"God, *what* are you trying to do to me? Can't you see I've reached my limit? I can't take any more of this confusion! What do you want from me Lord? I've just about had *enough*!" I screamed.

Backing into that truck was just the extra pound that broke the scale of my teetering emotions, and I didn't know how much more could I take. After the man I was supposed to marry left me for another woman, I got evicted from the apartment I had lived in for seven years, and then . . . well, just one thing after another, for twenty-four hours straight. I got a flat tire before I had a chance to buy a spare, and I broke two collector's dishes off a knickknack shelf at a house I was cleaning.

All those things happened shortly before my poor use of judgment while backing out of a very important parking lot—the site of my potential bread and butter.

I quieted down by the time I arrived at my brother's house, where I was staying. My body shivered with nervousness as I dialed the employer's phone number. I held back the lava of anxiety, rage, and frustration, trying to think what to say on the answering machine.

"I'm sorry, I was too embarrassed to tell you in person what happened when I left today. I backed into the pickup truck that was parked alongside your building. Please tell whoever owns it that I am sorry, and I hope you still want me to work for you." Then I hung up and began my wait for a response from the company. I felt like a criminal waiting for the verdict from a tough jury. I wondered if they would hire someone who just had an accident in their parking lot.

After obsessing about whether or not the company would reject me, I apprehensively predicted the response of the owner of the truck that I dented and smeared green paint all over. I was sure he would be very, very, upset.

Then suddenly I actually had one intelligent thought—the first in about a day and a half: I can't take back what happened. All I can do is pray.

So I began to ask God to forgive me for not trusting him fully with my future. I had been trying to take my life into my own hands by not letting God work out the details. I repented of all my sins of anger and worry and everything else I could think of. Then I began to reflect on all the times I couldn't see a way out of whatever circumstances I was facing and how God always came through for me.

I began to believe that perhaps God, who is bigger than all of us and the whole universe put together, still has a plan for my life, and it will happen for me no matter what I've done.

I suddenly felt encouraged that God can continue to work through me to help others despite my imperfections. I was soon to find out how much God really believes in me—a lot more than I believe in him!

A few days later, that employer called back and told me they had a job for me. Half of the weight of worthlessness I felt lifted. Then they told me that the person whose truck I hit was not that mad about it but at least wanted my phone number to talk to me about it.

In the meantime, I contacted my insurance company to try to make arrangements for repairing the truck. In the middle of waiting to hear from my insurance company, I received a call from the owner of the pickup. He told me he had decided not to do anything about it!

"Are you sure?" I asked in disbelief.

"Yeah, it's an old truck. It's not worth fixing," he said.

I was struggling a little with my pride at first, not wanting to "get off" so easy, but I knew that I would never be able to afford to pay for the dent myself if my insurance company refused to pay because of my missed payment last month, so I finally said, "Thank you—thank you very much!"

I was in shock, but I was also very grateful for this man's kindness and for God's mercy, which I felt was completely undeserved.

I was reminded of God's faithfulness to me despite outward circumstances and even despite my own poor judgment. I began to believe again that God loved me and that I can someday be a help to others, an encouragement to others, just as God and other people have been to me.

Most importantly of all, I began to believe in God once again. I thank God for his mercy and grace.

—*Julie A. Blodgett*

God Is on My Pillow

As I looked at him, lying there among the rumpled covers, I was reminded of an unfinished prototype, a mere skeleton that had yet to feel the miracle of a sculptor's hand. The sculptor had yet to add putty and substance to the frame and smooth the deep ridges of age away, to remove the pain of pending death from his furrowed brow, to put the color of life back, and to make my dad whole again.

Perfectly shaped orbs of brown surrounded by mottled yellow stared at me from darkened sockets with a faint sign of recognition. I thought I could detect the beginning of a smile crease his paraffin-white skin. A scrawny neck connected to an emaciated frame that produced no more than a large wrinkle in the sheets as evidence of its existence.

I stood transfixed in the open doorway of his bedroom, afraid to enter and afraid not to. I wondered what I could say that would not reveal the pity in my voice or hide the pain I felt. And how should

I act? Should I march straight to his bedside and crack a joke, as we had often done over the decades as father and son? Or should I approach him with pity—but pity for whom? Him or me? I decided to stand my ground in the middle and act neutral, say nothing, be the coward.

I walked over to his bed, brushed aside a few wispy strands of gray hair, and kissed his forehead. A tear found its way to a deep crease in his sunken cheek and followed it to the end, landing on his pillow. Was it a tear of sadness—for himself, for me, for us? Or was it a tear of happiness to be given the opportunity to meet with me one more time? The coward in me reared his ugly head again. I refused to admit that this might be our last meeting.

I sat with my dad from early in the afternoon until late into the night. As I held his hand, my mind went back to happier times. Times when a youthful smile creased a healthy face and when he laughed over some joke he had just told. Times when I felt just as much at home on his broad shoulders as I did when he tucked me into bed. I thought of all the trials and tribulations he had endured over the years, without complaint. I never saw him fret over an unpaid bill, the loss of a job, a sickly wife, or two wild teenagers. Did he pound his fist against some inert object in frustration when no one was looking? Did he weep behind closed doors over the sorrows of a hard life full of disappointment?

Did he ever take the Lord's name in vain and curse him in anger? Somehow I didn't think so. He was my rock, my foundation, and my hero.

I could sense a different rhythm in his breathing, a stronger heartbeat, and a blush of color on his cheeks. He will not die—I won't let him, I thought, but reality brought me to my senses. At least, I won't let him go until I've said a proper good-bye.

I gave Dad a gentle pat on the hand and left the room for a moment, closing the door behind me. When I returned, I could have sworn I distinctly heard two different voices from behind the closed door. I knocked lightly and entered, expecting to find someone else in the room, but it was empty, except for my dad. He read the confusion on my face and smiled. "You must think me a crazy old coot, son," he croaked. "I can assure you I'm not. Come, please sit down, there's a little story I feel compelled to tell you."

"But, Dad, should you—?"

"Nonsense, son, there'll be no secrets here. We both know where this is headed. I just feel I must tell you my little secret of life before I go. Come. Hold my hand like you were before. I'll need your strength to . . . "

His frail body shook from a gut-wrenching cough, and a small trickle of blood escaped his lips. He motioned me forward with a gnarled finger, and I dabbed a damp cloth on his parched lips, wiping the blood away.

The cough finally subsided, and he beckoned me closer, as a small child would to whisper a secret to his best friend.

"When I was little, I was very afraid of the dark," he began in a faint whisper. "I imagined all sorts of monsters and ghosts in my closet and under my bed. One night, during one of my paranoid episodes, my mother—your grandmother—sat next to me, like you are now, and told me this story of faith. 'Little one,' she said as she drew my fear-laden body to her, 'you must be the luckiest little boy in the whole wide world. Do you see that small indentation on your pillow? Well, that's God lying there beside you. He's there for one reason and one reason only, and that is to look after you, always. So, anytime you see a ghost or goblin, put your faith in God, talk it over with him, and it will go away.'

"She gently kissed my cheek and left the room. Over the years, I held to that faith. When things seemed to pile up and the burdens of life pressed down on me, God and I lay side by side on my pillow and talked it over. Those talks always saw me through and helped smooth out the rough parts of my life. You'd be surprised how many times God and I talked about you." He laughed, and another round of racking coughs seized his frail body.

When Dad drifted back to sleep again, I left the room to fill my coffee cup. When I entered the room once more, there was an unusually bright light over his bed. There, in the halo of light, I saw a deep indentation in his pillow. An angelic smile of blissful peace had replaced the lines in his face, etched there from endless hours of pain, and his arms were lovingly wrapped around his pillow.

To my knowledge, Dad never attended church, not in the true sense, but his chapel was his pillow. I was right all along: Dad did not die. He's in heaven, talking things over with God—on his pillow.

—*Stan Higley*

The Interview

I strode into the waiting area, my confident strides devouring carpeted real estate. I arrived fifteen minutes early for my interview for the position of fire captain, spurred on by career-advice maxims like "Arrive early" and "Dress like you already have the job," which were droning in my head as if from an implanted tape recorder.

I had agonized about what to wear, expending much time and thought before choosing my interview suit. "The strongest nonverbal statement you can make in the oral board is what you wear," said Captain Bob, fire service promotional guru. So I selected a double-breasted, charcoal gray suit, accentuated by white and gray pinstripes, paired with a white shirt, matching tie and handkerchief, and oxblood loafers.

My eye-popping ensemble, along with my fresh, high-and-tight haircut created a tumult among the secretaries. They acted like I'd leapt off the cover of *GQ* or *Ebony Men*.

"Lt. Greenwood, you look beautiful," said Joan. The other secretaries bustled around me, nodding in agreement.

A seasoned fire captain said, "You look great, Marc." His compliment startled me. Macho firefighters compliment one another about as often as Halley's comet appears.

As I awaited my call to the interview room, I reminisced. I had poured body, soul, and spirit into my efforts. I panted for this promotion, like the deer pants for thirst-quenching brooks. I wanted it. This interview was to complete the three-tiered promotional marathon, which included a 100–question, multiple-choice written exam, covering information culled from mountains of study material and an assessment center. Relentless in my pursuit for this promotion, I had driven myself preparing for the written exam, reading until my eyes burned and the pages blurred. I nailed that part of it, bagging a 94 percent during the morning session.

But I couldn't rejoice after the morning's success. I had to shift gears and brace myself for the afternoon session, which included the "in-basket" exercise. A question burned in my mind: Could I vault the "in-basket" hurdle? I dreaded it because I had bombed several practice sessions. Fire departments include these "in-basket" tests because experts consider the simulation to be an accurate predictor of managerial success. The exercise is designed to gauge a candidate's ability to identify problems, delegate, follow the chain of command, display interpersonal skills, and write memos in clear, concise language.

Proctors heaped documents onto my desk. I had forty-five minutes to read, decipher, prioritize, delegate, and document my resolution for each task in writing. Some tasks were simple, like scheduling a fire inspector to speak to the PTA. Other items dealt with ulcer-causing issues like sexual harassment or drinking on the job. I said a prayer and began.

Sweat-drenched, I completed my last task just as the proctor bellowed, "Time up!" But my exhaustion couldn't dampen my elation, because I experienced God's presence, illuminating my decision-making, providing salvos of insight, and sharpening my determination. My pencil scrawled orders, directives, and recommendations. I drove home, showered, ate, and prepared for the next day's session.

That session required me to display Solomon-like wisdom in unraveling a he-said, she-said riddle. I had to complete my investigation and present my recommendations while being videotaped. Video-taped sessions are tricky, because the camera magnifies and penalizes timid body language, an unkempt appearance, any nervous tics, or mangled speech.

But candidates who display decisiveness, exude a commanding presence, articulate advanced verbal skills, and maintain eye contact grab evaluators' attention.

As I continued to wait to be called for the final leg of this grueling marathon, I thought about the years preceding my captain's test. The department had been reconfigured. A new chief had been appointed, but he lacked the skills, knowledge, and ability to lead our department into the next century. Seven months earlier, he had rocked the department with a slew of capricious promotional decisions, in which ten top candidates with excellent service records were rejected for candidates scoring and ranking much lower.

This capsized the morale within the department, creating an environment of suspicion, anxiety, outrage, groveling, and envy. As the third-ranked candidate, I should have felt that this interview would be the prelude to glory and celebration for my promotion. Instead, I felt uneasy because rumors abounded that the chief approved of candidates backstabbing other candidates during their interviews. Certain rogue candidates would spew half-truths, fabrications, hearsay, and innuendo in their shameless pursuit of promotion at any cost. Their treachery validates this quote by A. W. Tozer: "What a man is under provocation is what he is. The mud must be at the bottom of the pool before it can be stirred up" (A. W. Tozer, *The Price of Neglect*, 1991).

Now that I was this close to the finish line, I was plagued by questions. Would I be able to stand the pressure once I got behind the closed door? Were my roots of righteousness entrenched? Soon I'd know. Meanwhile I immersed myself in my study cards.

"Lieutenant Greenwood, please come in," said the chief.

Whisked inside, I beheld a spacious room that was both a birth suite and a cemetery for promotional aspirations. The interview began with bland questions, questions that could have been answered by a cursory glance at my personnel folder. I'd scripted my professional accomplishments, and I was standing there eager to share the life experiences that would demonstrate my fitness for this position by verifiable accomplishments. I had served my community and department for eighteen years, risking life and limb, and here, on the cusp of my greatest achievement, I felt disrespected by such tomfoolery.

After all, according to *Ohio Employment Practices Law,* "the primary purpose of an interview is to obtain more detailed information about an applicant's qualifications. As such, the principal focus of the interview should be on exploring the details of an applicant's training or experience as they relate to the candidate's ability to perform the job."

"Lieutenant Greenwood, who was your worst officer, and why?"

Disgusted, I didn't answer. What was the relevance? What were they looking for? I'd scoured the nation, seeking education and increased professionalism. I had mentored firefighters who sought promotion, devoured industry magazines, and educated the public as I vied for promotion. My demeanor concealed the emotions that erupted within me. As house lieutenant and number three on the eligible list—as the person who assumes the captain's authority in his absence—I had maintained my paramedic certification for thirteen years. Why didn't they ask about that? I yearned to tell my story, introduce them to whom and what Marc D. Greenwood was about.

Instead, I fielded questions that were more of the same. "Lieutenant Greenwood, who is the best and worst candidate on the eligible list?"

The chief's personnel files detailed every significant event for each candidate, information that provided qualitative and quantitative data to make a job decision, if one were so inclined. He was responsible to evaluate those files. I refused to smear or praise other candidates. These questions mocked and insulted those who had competed according to the rules. The tenor of the interview plunged, growing contentious. Even though I could taste the promotion, I refused to make a mockery of my conscience.

I didn't get my promotion, but five years later I can still attest to this reality: "The best pillow is a clean conscience." My words of advice to Christians in the workplace is, prepare yourself for promotion. Move heaven and earth in the quest. But set boundaries. "Humble yourselves therefore under the mighty hand of God, that he may exalt you in due time" (1 Peter 5:6, KJV).

—Marc D. Greenwood

The Red
Polka-Dotted Cap

Like a groundhog wriggling out of his hole, the big burly man in the red polka-dotted cap squeezed himself out of my office door and lumbered toward his rusty old pickup truck. Staring through my window at the overall straps stretched across his broad shoulders, I thought, "What an eccentric old coot!"

Twenty-some years ago, I—barely what you'd call an adult—was the young pastor of an exciting new church. The church had seemed to rise up out of nowhere, like roadside flowers after a spring rain, and it was bursting at the seams with excited folks of every description. My dream had come true: God was using me. Full of enthusiasm—and myself—I concluded that all this wonderful success was mostly my doing. In other words, I was the perfect candidate for being taken down a notch or two, and God sent this bear of a man to do just that.

At that time, I was looking at myself through the little end of the telescope and at God through the big end. I had God all figured out. Why, he was totally predictable! You could look it up in those fancy theology books I bought to fill my office shelves. I was thoroughly convinced he only did certain things in certain ways through certain kinds of people. Boy, was my theological applecart about to be upset.

I was busy planning a Sunday school promotion when the giant stranger first knocked on my door. Welcoming him enthusiastically, I figured he was probably just another seeker, grateful to find our splendid new church. Declining my offer of a cup of coffee, he said, "I'll just get right to the point," as he eased his way into the chair across from my desk. Deep-set brown eyes twinkled in their wrinkled settings above swarthy cheeks covered in dark stubble. Leaning back and stretching his muddy brogans in front of him, he laced his sausage-like fingers together and rested them on the bib of his overalls as he peered at me from under the bill of that polka-dotted cap.

"I spend a lot of time praying," he announced, his massive body spilling over both sides of the chair. "God sent me here to warn you about some serious bumps in the road, dead ahead."

"Oh, really," I thought, looking him up and down. I hadn't seen him before, and I knew most everyone here in my hometown. Small towns don't have much inventory, so a newcomer stands out like a sunflower in the strawberry patch. And sometimes they're about as welcome, too.

I decided a few questions were in order. "What church did he attend?" "None." "What denominational faith did he claim?" "None in particular." "Did he know anyone in our church?" "Nope, God just put this on his heart." "Would he like to visit our church?" "Probably not, but he would be praying for me this week, because I was sure going to need it." With that, he was gone.

The visit troubled me, partly because it was so odd, but mostly because of his audacity. "Who did he think he was? He didn't even belong to a church, for heaven's sake." I knew that God just didn't do things this way, so I put the man and his red polka-dotted cap out of my mind and returned to my plans. "Hmmph," I thought. "The very idea of God sending some hillbilly stranger like that!"

Looking back, I realize I was suffering from a severe case of spiritual elitism. Oh, my bigotry didn't have anything to do with how well-off one was or even how well educated or socially connected. My uppity ecclesiastical attitude was based on orthodoxy, on doing things the way they'd always been done, on being spiritually correct.

Somehow, I'd failed to remember that Jesus didn't exactly recruit models of perfection. He chose rough-hewn fishermen and unscrupulous revenue agents, former prostitutes, and castoffs. Sure, they were changed by God's love, but on first glance—well, they probably looked a lot like this fellow with the red polka-dotted cap.

A few days after this visit, the roof of success and excitement over my up-and-coming ministry caved in. One of the prominent families of the church got mad and left in a big huff, kicking up plenty of dust in the process. I forgot all about "momentum" and just tried to control the damage. It was a difficult time, and the church lost several members. I wasn't even sure the infant congregation would survive. Suddenly I felt very alone.

Within a few weeks, things finally began to return to normal, and it looked like the church would survive. One day, I was praying when I remembered the man in the red polka-dotted cap. I mulled the memory over for a few seconds before putting him out of my mind. God just doesn't work that way, I thought. And besides, if God had something to tell me, he would have chosen a more worthy messenger.

A little over a year later, the church was healthy again when guess who showed up? Yep, Mr. Polka Dot. This time his visit wasn't so mysterious, and we became better acquainted. With a friendly smile, he explained that he was a blacksmith and welder, hence the polka-dotted cap, a symbol of the trade. He had recently moved to our area from California and lived way out in the woods. He made his living building operating-scale steam engine trains, big enough for rich men to ride atop and puff around their fancy estates on the West Coast.

Again, he said that he prayed for me often. And again, God told him troubles were around the bend for me, but God would see me through. We talked a little theology, his a bit eccentric, but not quite heretical, and with a wink, he was gone.

Sure enough, in a few days, a crisis erupted. And sure enough, God saw me through. To make a long story short, over the next few years, every time I was about to face a crisis, that polka-dotted cap appeared at my office door. In one way, I dreaded seeing him roll his hulking frame out of his pickup truck, because it meant trouble was coming. But in another way, his visits were a comfort, because I knew God was watching over me.

After a while he stopped coming by, and I never saw him again. But I know he was real, because I ran into a local steel merchant who verified the strange character and his strange occupation. He said one day the man just picked up—lock, stock, and steam engine—and moved away.

Why had God put such a strange man in my path? I've decided he did it to let me know how much he loves me. He cares about what is going on in my life, and when troubles come, he'll see me through.

I learned another lesson, too. God could have sent his assurance in a much more conventional way through a much more common person. I think God used such a strange messenger to knock some holes in my spiritual prejudice. If God could use an eccentric named John the Baptist who wore a camel's-hair coat and munched on locusts, he could use a big fellow who wore a red polka-dotted cap.

Sometimes it's difficult to see God at work. But my friend with the polka-dotted cap taught me a wonderful lesson. Even when I feel alone, God is right by my side. He's in the tender touch of my loving wife and the hearty laugh of a friend. He's in the kind gesture of a stranger and the pleasant smile of a child. God uses all sorts of people to pass on his word.

In the same way, God sent us the gift of his son in a common wrapper, a man named Jesus. And God is still sending gifts of love and assurance. Some arrive in shiny, store-bought finery, topped with satin bows. But some are covered with rough brown paper and tied with cotton string. The wrapper doesn't matter; it's what's inside that counts. Even more important is the One who sent the gift. I almost missed a wonderful gift from God, just because it came wrapped in a red polka-dotted cap.

—Dean Mailes

Most High Connections

I was nineteen years old, completely bald, and getting ready to have brain surgery. My life seemed like it was over. I was hoping I would either wake up to find myself in heaven or wake up to find that it was all a nightmare.

But while I was planning for the end of my life, God was getting ready to reveal his plans for me.

During the operation on my brain, I actually left my body. I was not scared; instead I was filled with peace and love. I knew it wasn't a dream—I felt the coolness of the wind and the roughness of the concrete steps going up to the front door of my mom and dad's house. I was standing there, not knowing why I wasn't in heaven and believing God didn't even want me, and then I saw Jesus. I felt such joy when he reached out his hand to me.

Jesus said, "Come with me. I have something to show you." Jesus said that when I looked back on my life on the times I thought I was alone, He was there with me. He was protecting me, saving me from death, caring for me, loving me always. But I was never looking up at him. Then I felt I was being lifted in Jesus' arms. It was like going through a time capsule that was my life. All the times I wanted to forget were times when I had every reason to stop and praise God, not turn away from Him. I have been in some tight spots in my life. I could have been stabbed, shot, beaten to death, and left for dead, but that was not my fate.

Then my feet touched the ground, and I was somewhere I'd never been before. I knew I wanted to stay forever. Then I heard the voice of God. I felt every word through my whole body like electricity. It sounded like many waterfalls. I covered my eyes, the light was so bright. I fell to my knees. And God told me that it wasn't my time to die. There was too much work left to be done. God had more important plans for my life—to be a blessing in the world. I was worth more to God alive than dead and serving no more purpose in the world. He said that I had a lot of love to give, and I was to use that love to touch other people and bless them with the gifts that he has given to me.

When I woke up, I was in the recovery room. I hadn't died, and I knew that what I had experienced was very real. Everything God said to me about my life was going to come true. When I was taken to my regular room, my brother, his girlfriend, and my older sister came in to see me. Everyone was so upset, but I couldn't figure out why. Maybe it was because I looked like a mummy or because they knew I didn't have a strand of hair under all those bandages. All I know is that I was just starting to be happy.

God made me happier than I ever thought I could be. He gave me a wonderful husband, and we have been happily married for sixteen years. I have a beautiful relationship with the Lord, which has produced the incredible gifts that I needed to reach millions of people. God was right when he said I had a lot of love to give. I love Jesus and Jim so much, and not being able to give birth to a child, I believe I am able to love even more people. I have so much extra love that I can't possibly share it all with just my family!

God blessed me all those years ago, and he blesses me more every day. I believe in my heart that he wants others to feel that same love. That is why I follow the commandments Jesus told us to live by, next to loving the Lord God with all our hearts, souls, and minds. He also told us to love our neighbor as ourselves (Matthew 22:37-40). I am a lover of people. I love people who don't even know me but have blessed me with their Christian walk. From single moms who struggle to give their children the best they can, to missionaries who sacrifice their lives to spread the good news to a lost world. I love all the people God has brought into my life. I even love my enemies, like Jesus did.

At times it feels like too much of a burden, but it is one I gladly bear because of God's love for me. I love the blessing and privilege of praying and interceding for everyone. It does not matter whether a person is bad or good—everyone can be blessed in a relationship with him. The special gift that God has given me with which to bless others is the gift of scriptural poetry. It has inspired people to apply his word to their daily lives. As for me, I am going to continue to share my love with other people through my ministry, "Most High Connections," because that is what the Lord has asked me to do.

—Carol D. Hoener

Without a Doubt

To some, faith is only a word. To my grandmother, it was a way of life. She was a spiritual matriarch who lived humbly and taught her family to never give up but always believe the impossible. She taught us not only in words but in the life she lived. She epitomized faith. Whenever I face an impossible situation, I can still hear her sweet voice speaking to me: "Believe, dear heart, just believe." She addressed all her grandchildren by that endearing term. It made each of us feel special. And that was nothing short of amazing when you consider how many of us grandkids there are. She never faltered in the face of adversity, but she always exuded faith, ever pushing her way through a mobbing crowd of obstacles. I have no memories of my grandmother ever voicing doubt in God. To her, faith was as simple as breathing. It was her way of life, even when others may have thought it would seem easier to just give up.

As a young wife she had been abandoned, left alone to raise her ten children, just at the end of the Depression that created difficult times for even the strongest and wealthiest. Her faith and prayers carried her and her young family through those hard days. She welcomed each morning the same—on her knees before God, praying for each individual member of her family as well as her pastor, neighbors, and politicians. With ten children (and years later, twenty-two grandchildren, several great-grandchildren, and a bounty of in-laws, nieces, and nephews), you could count on breakfast being served just before noon.

One story of her deep faith serves as a hallmark and continues to be repeated among our family members today. Once when her children (my mother among them) were very small, work was scarce, and she had spent all of her earned income for rent. There was only a small amount of flour in the cupboard. She awoke that morning as usual, falling to her knees in prayer. She reminded God that there was little food in the house and asked him to work a miracle. Then in complete faith she thanked God for the miracle and began her day.

She baked the humble amount of flour into biscuits that morning. With each knead of the dough, she continued to thank God for a miracle. After the children gobbled up the biscuits, they went carefree about their play as she carried on with her housework. Dusk appeared, and as she liked to tell it, "The little ones began to wander into the house from playing outside, and they told me they were hungry. I asked them to be patient, and I explained we would all eat shortly. I knew there was no more food left in the cupboard. But I also knew that wasn't a problem for God. He would provide."

The day was swiftly fading, and soon she would need to prepare food for her hungry children. Then, just as she had expected, there came a knock at the door. When she opened it, she saw three gentlemen from her church, arms full of groceries. They said they hoped she didn't mind, but they had purchased far too many groceries and wanted to know if she would take some off their hands. She smiled and thanked them, saying she had been expecting them.

Later, as an adult and a mother myself, I asked her how her faith could have been so strong when she knew that her children were hungry. What if God hadn't come through? I'll never forget her reply: "Dear heart, it never crossed my mind to doubt. God's love is greater than our doubt."

In 1997 when she passed away, all her children and grandchildren were at her bedside, adoringly paying tribute to her devotion and strength. Even to the end, she reminded us that faith would carry us through the most difficult of times.

In the years since my grandmother's death, many challenging obstacles have been hurled my way. Life, I've learned, does not discriminate. It rains on the good and the bad. There have been many times I have had to remind myself of grandmother's undying faith and her loving prayers. When my family experienced the sudden death of my young sister-in-law, I had to remind myself of it. When my father-in-law became terminally ill with cancer, I had to remind myself of it. When a precious aunt died of lupus, I had to remind myself of it. When I suddenly and unexpectedly joined the ranks of the unemployed, for yet a second time within two years, I had to remind myself of it. When my family experienced great financial loss, I had to remind myself of it. When I was bombarded with medical bills from an untreatable medical condition, I had to remind myself of it.

I have seen how life can change abruptly and, without any given notice, become very difficult. I have often struggled to put on a happy face and pretend all is well, while inside my heart was hurting deeply. It seems when you get to the point that you think it can't get any harder, life deals you yet another blow. It's at those times, in the depths of my despair, that I have longed to pick up the phone and hear my grandmother's voice speaking to me: "It will be all right, dear heart."

My sweet mother, who also shares a deep faith, assures me God will take care of everything. I choose to believe her. Somewhere deep inside, in a place of quiet reserve, I do believe, because I have seen faith in action. It has been a great gift. I also believe that my grandmother's prayers, then and now, continue to go before us, keeping us all close to the very heart of God. I often find myself quoting the old adage, "This too shall pass." And the strange thing is, it does.

The Bible tells us that faith is the substance of the very things we hope for when we don't yet see the evidence of it. I think my grandmother would put that in more simple terms: "Believe. Just believe, dear heart. God's love is greater than our doubts."

—*Mary Catherine Rogers*

A Ten-Dollar Lunch

The whitefish was broiled beautifully and was flanked by sides of rice and peas in a light tomato sauce. My waiter's parting words were, "Please enjoy." Well, enjoy I did; my lunch was delectable. I consumed all the food, which was unusual for me.

With the arrival of my bill, the clock on the wall confirmed it was time to return to work. I prepared myself to enter the cold again, put two dollars on the table, and gave the host a twenty-dollar bill for my seven-dollar lunch. My change went into my coat pocket.

The streets in Greektown were not very busy, though I navigated through a small group of people in front of Fishbone's. I said hello as they made eye contact but paid no particular attention to anyone.

Continuing down Brush Street, I encountered more people in front of the Atheneum Hotel. A man and a lady with a cane approached from the opposite direction. They walked past the group of people and, to my surprise, came directly to me. The man stepped up to me, looked me in the eye, and said, "Excuse me, Miss, but will you help us? Anything you give us will be appreciated, anything at all; please?" The man's request seemed more on the lady's behalf than his own. The lady stood in place, silently clutching her cane. The lack of space between them revealed her vulnerability and dependence on him.

I shook my head no and said, "I'm sorry, but I don't have anything with me." He thanked me, and the lady politely nodded and smiled as he returned to her side. He pulled her arm through his, and they went on their way. I continued on my separate path.

At the next street corner, my spirit was nagged by discontent, and I heard "You know they need me." The words seemed to invade my psyche, as if the money in my pocket were speaking to me. It cried out to go with the lady and man. The entire scenario replayed in my mind in vivid detail and slow motion as I relived what happened.

The man was tall and skinny. His hair was wild, like Don King's, only shorter. The lenses in his glasses were as thick as pop bottles. His blue overcoat was old and more suited for cool fall weather than for the wintry temperatures of the day. He had no gloves or scarf. His black shoes were old and worn. His brown trousers were dirty and wrinkled.

The plump lady wore a short, drab green coat, a brown wool hat, and brown wool mittens. Her straight, mousy brown hair hung to her shoulders from under the hat. The cane she clutched was white with a red tip. Her eyes were set back in her pale face and shut tight, like they had never been open. Clearly she was blind.

My heart pounded as I realized what I had done. The voice of the money in my pocket sounded loud: "What can they do? Where can they go? Who's going to help them?"

I urgently wanted to put the money in the man's hand. I turned around to find the couple, but they where nowhere to be seen. I walked back to the Atheneum Hotel but didn't find them. I walked up Lafayette Street but didn't see them. I checked my watch. It was already two o'clock, and my lunch hour was over.

I headed back to work feeling dejected and convicted. The money in my pocket spoke its disapproval again: "What difference will these few dollars make to you? Why didn't you help them?" I had no answer to the questions. I only had guilt and shame.

Every day after that, I looked for the couple wherever I went to lunch. I kept extra money in my pocket—ten, fifteen, or twenty dollars. I routinely walked through Greektown, but I didn't see the man with the lady. One, then two weeks passed, and I continued my campaign to find the two. I prayed for forgiveness at the missed opportunity and for another chance. This couple needed one friendly face in the crowd. I didn't know that face should have been mine, and I only recognized it when it was too late.

Four weeks passed following my encounter with destiny, but I still went walking during lunch in ready mode, ever hopeful, ever watchful.

For reasons only God knows, on one particular day I was late leaving the office. It was one-thirty by the time I bundled up for my lunchtime walk in the cold. I went outside at Randolph. It was sunny, so I reached for my sunglasses. After several deep breaths and feeling the rays of the sun, a calm engulfed me. I headed toward Greektown.

The light at the corner of Randolph and Larned held a steady signal, Do Not Walk. Traffic was heavy, so I waited and surveyed the pedestrians. Slowly, the couple standing across the street came into focus. There they were, and I was ready. Removing my glove, I put my right hand in my pocket and clutched the money. My heart jumped for joy!

When the light changed, I didn't move. Things went into slow motion. The man guided the lady across the street. She seemed so dependent on him, and he seemed so determined to protect her. They walked directly to me. Before he could say anything, I took his hand and looked him in the eye. The bills went happily into his hand as I said, "This is for you." I smiled and hid tears behind my glasses.

The sun felt warm as I continued to walk. Half a block away I heard a loud voice calling from behind me. I heard the voice again. The third time I turned around. It was the man. He and the lady were awkwardly running toward me. I stopped and saw tears running down his face as he approached. "Thank you so much! God bless you and your family." The words came from a place deep in his soul and went deep into mine.

Putting both my hands around his, I let the tears flow. "He already has; and God bless you two." The sun felt even warmer when I saw the smile on the lady's face.

The amount of money I placed in the man's hand was small, only ten dollars. What we got for those ten dollars was worth far more.

I still walk downtown during my lunch with an extra ten or twenty dollars in my pocket, and I still look for that couple. I've made a promise to help them whenever we have another encounter. But I have yet to see them again.

—*M. Lee Brown*

 Evidence of Life

I couldn't go into that hospital room anymore. I didn't want my thirty-one-year-old daughter to be disturbed by my hysterical crying. I leaned against a wall in a vacant waiting room and sobbed, "Where are you, God?"

Carolyn was dying. The lymphoma had been diagnosed only two months earlier. Now she also had leukemia. Tumors had spread to her liver, and pneumonia was taking her into respiratory arrest. My husband stayed by her bed singing hymns and praying. In a few hours, she was gone.

Carolyn died with faith in her heart and a prayer on her lips, but along with my grief, doubt shot through my brain. Do we really have hope beyond the grave? I wasn't as sure as before. I returned from Carolyn's funeral with a desire to look at the evidence concerning life beyond physical death, using my skills as a newspaper reporter.

I began to examine the Bible. I looked again at eyewitnesses' writings about Jesus Christ's resurrection and the Christian hope of eternal life. I knew the Bible well, but I needed to study its teachings again.

Perhaps because I am a health and religion writer, I also decided to look for evidence in the human body indicating that we are more than flesh. Is there something eternal residing inside us that lives even though our body dies?

I interviewed a neurologist who diagnoses brain death. I did several stories on the human genome—our chromosomes and cell genetics. Like a diagnostic laparoscopic instrument going through digestive plumbing, I journeyed through many a medical expert's brain, searching for facts about health, life, and death. I observed and interviewed the sick and dying.

I began to think about how parts of our body can be cut away or can die, but we continue to live and be the same person. Every day people have gall bladders, livers, kidneys, breasts, or limbs removed in surgery or accidents. We can even have someone else's body parts or organs inserted into us, yet we remain the same person. Although brain function is a determinant of life, parts of the brain can be removed while the body still lives, and we remain who we are. Furthermore, the 75 trillion cells in the human body are constantly dying and being replaced. Our skin is rebuilt every seven days. Cells in the lining of the intestine die after a day and a half; white blood cells after thirteen days; red blood cells after 120 days. Remaining cells divide to replenish themselves. With the exception of the nervous system, which includes the brain, our bodies "die" many times throughout our lifetimes.

Until recently, it was thought that brain cells and other cells in the central nervous system were gone once they died. But a special report in the *Denver Post* by *New York Times* writer Holcomb B. Noble on October 30, 1998, said that new growth of brain cells has been discovered in the hippocampus, a center of learning and memory in the brain.

In addition to what happens with our cells, we remain the same individual throughout our lifetime, despite growth, weight gain, and weight loss. We lose weight, and it disappears as we burn it, exhale it, or excrete it. Lost weight used to be flesh and blood. Yet no one ever grieves over it. Instead, we rejoice when it is gone.

Our inner self—the human soul and spirit—remains, while our body constantly changes. But after the body is completely dead, will the person we are still live on?

Jesus made the startling statement, "Whoever lives and believes in me will never die." So I searched the Bible about Jesus' resurrection. The Book of Acts hinges on the Resurrection. No one found a body.

Historians tell us the disciples, who at first couldn't believe Jesus rose from the grave, died for their faith because they believed Jesus was alive. Who would die for something they knew was a lie?

Earlier, Jesus demonstrated his power over death by resurrecting Lazarus from the grave, although Lazarus had been dead four days. John wrote about being an eyewitness to such events. "We have seen with our eyes, we have examined and our hands have touched," he wrote. Luke, a physician, also pointed out that he was an eyewitness. The apostle Peter wrote, "We have not followed cunningly devised fables . . . but were eyewitnesses of his majesty."

In the Apostle Paul's letter to Timothy, Paul said Jesus abolished death and brought life and immortality to light through the gospel. He compares death to a seed planted in the ground that will grow and live with a new body.

Yet living forever is still sometimes difficult for me to comprehend. Most of us fear the death of our loved ones or ourselves. We're not alone in this. In his book *Facing Death and the Life After*, evangelist Billy Graham tells about a time when he came near death and was afraid of it. He had already undergone one surgery and needed another to save his life. "I can remember alternating between complete peace in knowing that I would be with my Lord Jesus Christ, and a fear of leaving my loved ones. Neither emotion predominated, but I seemed to vacillate back and forth."

In another example from the Bible, King Hezekiah became ill, and God sent the prophet Isaiah to tell him he was going to die. Hezekiah said, "In the prime of my life must I go through the gates of death and be robbed of the rest of my years? I cried like a swift or thrush, I moaned like a mourning dove. My eyes grew weak as I looked to the heavens. I am troubled; O Lord, come to my aid!"

Even Jesus was uncomfortable with his imminent death, possibly because he knew how he would suffer. Jesus prayed, "O my Father, if it be possible, let this cup pass from me" (Matthew 26:38, KJV).

Fear of death is common not only because death could be painful, but it separates us from earth. Also death is something we don't fully understand. Yet death isn't that much different from birth. Do we really understand how we got here? Do we understand how our lives began as a human egg, a tiny speck, fertilized with a tiny sperm—a life that develops into a beautiful baby to be born, grow, walk on earth, die, and pass into eternity?

Although I don't fully comprehend it all, I found peace and comfort from my studies of life and death. Did my search prove we will live forever? No. My search brought me back to something I already knew. Every theory or belief about how we got here on earth and where we're going takes faith. None of it can be proved. Even belief in God requires faith. I am to believe if I do not wish to perish but have everlasting life.

I choose to believe.

—*Ada Nicholson Brownell*

A Piece of Blue Ribbon

One more snip and the ribbon fell free into my hand. A ribbon so blue it was almost purple, so thin that light filtered through. A piece only twenty-six inches long. Yet this piece of blue ribbon represented hours of agonizing, tearful prayers to God on behalf of a mission in India dedicated to rescuing infant girls from infanticide. My heart swelled with love and thankfulness to God, who hears and answers prayers in just the way he desires for the good of those who are praying.

It was a warm, cloudless February day in Chennai, India. It was a day I'll never forget. "Thank you, God," my heart sang in love and gratitude.

This all started a year before, when my husband and I decided to go to India to observe the mission work we had been supporting at the World Bible College, which was overseen by Paul Renganathan and his wife, Dorothy. We never imagined what a life-changing experience that journey would be.

Paul met us at the airport and took us to his house. We would also visit many villages in India. And we soon realized that we would not be treated simply as tourists here; we were part of Paul's team, and we would be treated as Paul's equals. We were overwhelmed by the welcome and honors bestowed on us, although we felt so unworthy. The people were so hospitable, sharing whatever they had. They honored us with garlands of jasmine flowers and leis of roses. They adorned us with wool shawls.

Men and women were hungry to hear the gospel of Jesus. They worked all day, walked several miles to the service at Paul's mission, sat for up to three hours cross-legged on the ground, walked back home, and cooked their evening meal. I could see God in their eyes, on their faces, and in their smiles. Their singing lifted my spirit to heaven. I felt so close to God.

We learned about the mission work. We saw the orphanages, with so many happy, thriving children. We were welcomed into the preachers' homes. We were shown love and respect beyond measure. My heart was filled with joy and love for the people in India.

The time to leave that beautiful country came all too soon. The night we said our good-byes, Paul told us about the infanticide of little girls and of his goal to open an orphanage for fifty babies. It would be called the Ruth Foundation. I was ecstatic. This would be my goal, too.

I returned home ready to get the mission built. We were to receive some money from an investment—more than a half million dollars—so I would see that the babies were rescued.

But I soon found out that God had other ideas. Our investment money was lost in a scam. Now what?

At first I wasn't too worried. God had always been there for me. So I prayed. "OK, God. I know it's your will that these babies not be killed. It's happening, God, even now. Please, let us get the money."

The answer I received was, "Babies have been killed for centuries. Babies were killed when Moses was born. Babies were killed when the Israelites left Egypt. Babies were killed when Jesus was born. I know what I'm doing."

"But, God," I said with all the urgency that I could deliver, "Paul can't build the mission without my money. Please, in any way you can, let us get the money."

"It's my mission, not yours, Ruth. I will see it to completion, with or without you," was the answer that came to me.

Everything came into perspective. I had to admit I was overzealous. I had left God's power and my faith out of the mission.

I fell to my knees and begged for God's forgiveness. I prayed for increased faith and that he would help me to get out of his way. I felt so guilty that my pride and lack of faith had hindered the building of the mission.

My sister had passed away and left her living sisters a percentage of her money. I could send Paul some money, but not enough.

"God," I prayed, "if you're not going to let us get the money now, then please provide money from some other source."

Finally I turned the mission totally over to God, having faith that he knew best. I prayed continually for the Ruth Foundation, that all would go according to God's will. I also sent boxes of pencils, candy, crayons, books, and clothing to the mission. I decided to do all I could for the children in India.

Before long, we received an e-mail that the boys' home, another part of the Ruth Foundation, was ready to be opened.

"God," I prayed. "I want to go back. I want to be there when it opens. Please, God, provide a way."

"Go," I heard.

"What?" I said.

"Just go!" I heard again.

I was in awe. "Thank you, God," I prayed, not knowing if the trip was really possible.

When my husband came to bed, I said, "Do you think we could scrape enough money together to go back to India?"

Without hesitation he said, "I'll check things out in the morning."

Wow! I praised God until I fell into a very restful sleep.

In the morning, my husband started checking for the cheapest airfare. We soon had our date for departure, and we were on our way.

Shortly after we arrived, we were on our way to the boys' home of the Ruth Foundation. It was completed. They had added two rooms to the church building for the five boys who would live there. My joy was almost uncontainable. A dream come true!

We drove further on, and the driver stopped at a set of double iron gates. Down the lane, lined with plants and fruit trees, was a very nice building. Paul said, "This is the girls' orphanage, which will be part of the Ruth Foundation. The men are working as fast as they can to get it completed before you have to go back to the U.S. We will have the grand opening, and you can cut the ribbon."

I was speechless. My heart sang praises to God. "I knew you could and would complete this orphanage, God, in your own way and according to your time, not mine. Thank you for letting me be a part of my dream—your mission."

I could not believe this was happening. I could not fathom that the orphanage was actually built. It was incredible. I could not put my thoughts into words. My emotions were on hold. All my hopes and dreams were before my eyes—turned into reality.

A few days later, I stood on one side of the door of the girls' orphanage, scissors poised, ready to cut the blue ribbon—the greatest fulfillment of my life.

On our last night in India, over a meal with Paul and Dorothy, I confessed to them my overzealous attitude about the mission. "I wanted things my way. We were unable to send you as much money as we wanted you to have."

Dorothy raised her eyes to mine even though she did not lift her head from eating. Her fingers full of food were poised in the air. Paul sat with a stunned look. I thought they were angry with me. Instead, in his calm, controlled voice, Paul said, "The property for the orphanage was God's provision. I had talked to the previous owner, and he thought he needed more money than what we had offered. Months after that, he called me back to talk about the sale. I was praying on the next Friday. Normally my cell phone would be switched off during prayer and meetings, but that day it was accidentally left on. My banker called me and asked if I needed a loan. He told me if I took the loan before the end of October, he would not charge any loan documentation fee. I asked him when I should come to the bank. He told me the bank representative was coming to my office in two hours with the needed forms. He brought them, and

I signed. Getting a loan in India is a big deal and very time consuming, but the money was available the next day. The bank didn't know I was looking for property. God did."

Chills went up my spine. Our faithful God provided everything in his own time and his own way. With my faith restored and a heart full of joy, I was ready to return home.

—*Ruth I. Danner Wilson*

The Christmas Cactus

A Christmas cactus is a spiky, spindly thing. Like many people, it's more "cactus" than "Christmas" most of the time. A friend gave me one a few years ago, even though I don't exactly have a green thumb.

Little acts of kindness meant a lot to me back then. Our son, Tim, was going to jail.

My husband, Denny, and I have five children. Tim was our first. He was a sweet-natured and outgoing kid, growing up. You couldn't help but love Tim.

High school was rough on Tim because we moved the summer before his senior year. He started college but dropped out and became an insurance agent. He was really good at it. He never had to "sell himself." People just naturally gravitated to him.

Then out of nowhere, Tim began to make money. Suddenly he was buying and selling land. He opened jewelry stores and a women's clothing store. He drove a Mercedes and bought one for Denny and me.

Then one night the phone rang. It was Tim's girl-friend. She was frantic. Tim was in a hotel room. He was going to kill himself. I drove through the rain to find him and bring him home.

That night, Tim told Denny and me that there was no more money, that none was coming in—that he was involved in criminal activity. Together, we decided to call the FBI. They came and took Tim's confession.

It turned out that Tim's real estate business was a pyramid scheme that cost hundreds of good people their life savings. The thing Tim feared most was about to happen—he was sentenced to prison for eight years.

Tim wrote to us about his first night in jail: "When we reached the cell, one guard removed the only light bulb, saying, 'We wouldn't want you to hurt yourself, would we?' The other guard shoved me through the cell door. It was like being in a damp, dreary basement. The walls were covered with per-verted poetry, crosses, initials, and every imaginable curse word. A blistering cold wind blew through a hole in the window, high up, along the top of the wall. I could see my breath."

I didn't know how I was going to handle having Tim so far away, locked up in the cold and dark, facing ugly and terrifying things. Moms are always the ones who help their children at such times. But I couldn't be there for him. If only I could have sat on his bunk with him, praying and reminiscing about old times. If only I could have hugged him and told him that everything would be all right.

But life goes on. Denny and I went about our day-to-day lives with "game faces" and heavy hearts. Whenever we could, we'd drive the 200 miles to visit Tim on weekends. Then on those Monday mornings, we'd pull ourselves together and go to work. Denny was a manager at Bell Labs. I had a Christian counseling practice. Many of my clients were adults who'd been abused as children. Sometimes their sadness, combined with my own, was almost too much to bear.

Then something wonderful began to happen. In prison, Tim began Bible studies. He started leading the prison choir. He directed the men in several plays about a character called "Arch the Angel." He played Santa for the prison staff and the community. Because of his love of children, Tim makes a wonderful Santa.

Before long, Tim was counseling many of his fellow prisoners, including the last of the Hatfields, as in the "Hatfields and McCoys" feud. On my second visit to the prison, a man came up to me and said, "If it weren't for your son, I'd be dead by now. I was going to take my life, but I met Tim, and he prayed with me. Things haven't been the same since."

Tim started writing inspirational stories based on his experiences in jail. With his dad's help, he sent them to friends and relatives and to a radio station that had an outreach program for prisoners.

Tim also helped his fellow prisoners get their GED (General Education Development) certificates. This was something he really enjoyed, and it was one of his proudest accomplishments. He was giving these men more than a diploma—he was giving them hope.

Some miraculous things happened to Tim, too. Admittedly, he had gone to prison with a lot of baggage. He had been arrogant, hotheaded, and materialistic. But prison changed him for the better. He stopped rationalizing and realized that he was getting the punishment he deserved for all the hurt he had caused. His letters told us how much he was learning: to contain his anger; to give with a cheerful heart; to live one day at a time. He even faced up to his weight problem and lost 140 pounds!

Tim's fellow inmates wrote to me, too. Those letters were such a comfort. As difficult as those times were for all of us, I knew that Tim was where he was needed—and where he needed to be.

Around this time, a friend noticed my cactus. It was four years old by now, somewhat bedraggled but still alive. My friend asked how often it flowered. I was surprised: "This plant is supposed to flower?"

"Yes," she said, "it's a Christmas cactus. They have beautiful blossoms."

I discovered that to get the cactus to bloom, you're supposed to lock it in a closet for about six weeks. No light, no heat, no water until buds form—with luck, around Christmastime. So that's what I did. I had no expectations; I just hoped it would survive.

A month and a half later, there were large pink buds on several of the cactus's branches. Sure enough, it was flowering. As I looked at it in amazement, my heart soared. My Christmas cactus was just like Tim. He had been locked away in a cold, dark place, but he had blossomed. His life had become truly beautiful.

Tim was released from prison in 1995, and he continues to grow and thrive. He earned a B.A. from the Philadelphia College of the Bible and is now a gifted minister and inspirational speaker. He married a wonderful young woman named Gina, and they have two little girls. We spend every Christmas together.

—*Carol F. Mog with Patricia Bridgman*

 Contributors

Linda E. Allen ("Blessed with Less") is the author of *Decking the Halls* and *Menagerie at the Manger*. She writes inspirational, nostalgic, and nature books, articles, and essays.

Janet M. Bair ("The Missing Jewel") is a freelance writer and a children's librarian. She is the author of the book *Devotions for Young Readers* as well as many other articles and stories. She lives in Ansonia, Connecticut, with her husband and two daughters, Joanna and Emily.

Larry Baker ("The Miracle Man") is a hairstylist who works and ministers to young people in downtown Fort Collins, Colorado. God's love daily changes the lives of those Larry encounters.

Alma Barkman ("In His Hands") is a freelance writer and photographer from Winnipeg, Canada. She is the author of six books, and her work appears in various publications, including *Daily Guideposts*. She and "friend hubby" have four children, and eight grandchildren.

Angela Batchelor ("My Day in Court"), author of *The Other Side of Motherhood* and *Mercy on the Journey*, is a teaching literary artist in Fishkill, New York, and contributes to *Gannett Poughkeepsie Journal*'s Family Weekend Planner.

Julie A. Blodgett ("Beyond Frustration") was born and raised in Wisconsin. She has been writing ever since high school as a creative relief from life's pressures.

Cindy Boose ("Following God's Lead") is an Army wife, home-school teacher, and mother of four teenage daughters. Her work has appeared in *Grit* and *Women Alive!* magazines, as well as *The Front Porch* syndication.

Elaine L. Bridge ("In the Driver's Seat of God's Love" and "Woodpecker King") is a former forester. She now spends her time developing her relationship with God, caring for her husband and three sons, and writing inspirational material.

Patricia Bridgman ("The Christmas Cactus"), a retired public relations manager, now writes for children. Her articles appear in *Highlights, Cricket, Spider, Girls' Life*, and other publications.

Ada Nicholson Brownell ("Evidence of Life") is a freelance writer in Springfield, Missouri. She spent seventeen years as a newspaper reporter in Colorado. She and her husband, Lester, have four married children and one daughter in heaven.

M. Lee Brown ("A Ten-Dollar Lunch") resides in metro Detroit. She also wrote the foreword to *Ella's Cuisine*, a salt-, sugar-, and wheat-free cookbook and is currently writing a novel.

Connie Sturm Cameron ("Mommy, What Happens When We Die?") is a freelance writer. This story is excerpted from her book *God's Gentle Nudges*, available at *www.pleasantword.com*. To contact her, send mail to P.O. Box 30, Glenford, OH 43739 or e-mail to conniec@netpluscom.com.

Yvonne Curry Smallwood ("A Lesson in Benevolence"), who resides in Upper Marlboro, Maryland, credits God and her family for each opportunity to share her published stories and essays.

Virginia Dawkins ("Scary Places") has been published in *A Cup of Comfort Devotional* and is a columnist for two newspapers in Meridian, Mississippi.

Matthew Nelson Drumheller ("Speaking of Faith…") is a college instructor of communication and religion. He writes inspirational stories and draws cartoons. Matthew authored thirty articles for national encyclopedias and is currently writing a religious fiction thriller called *The Ledger.*

Kriss Erickson ("Disturbing the Waters") is a versatile freelance writer who has had over 300 items published since she began writing professionally in 1981. She has often illustrated her work or provided photographs when needed.

Devon France ("Cathedral Building") is a middle school teacher from the Los Angeles area who loves her two daughters and writing inspirational stories, both fiction and nonfiction.

Sherri Fulmer Moorer ("The Evil of Conformity" and "Not Your Average Joe (or Jane)") is a Christian writer from Columbia, South Carolina, and is the author of *Battleground Earth—Living by Faith in a Pagan World*.

Rita S. Galieh ("The Power of Touch") is a scriptwriter and co-presenter on an Australian Christian radio program. She also regularly ministers in Southeast Asian Buddhist prisons, hospitals, schools, and the Y.W.C.A.

Mary Gallagher ("A Whisper in the Lilacs") is a reading teacher and a writer who lives in southern Ohio with her husband and two healthy sons. She continues to listen for God's voice in the everyday moments of life.

Nancy N. Gates ("Amazing Grace") is a freelance writer who has enjoyed many cranberry-scented autumns at home in Alaska with her husband, Chris, six children, and two grandchildren.

Marc D. Greenwood ("The Interview") is married to Deborah and has four adult sons. His work has been published in numerous national trade and Christian publications.

Linda R. Henson ("Smarts Aren't Enough") has published works in various anthologies, magazines, and newspapers. She is an Assemblies of God minister, the director of Global University–ICI, Bahamas, and a former language arts teacher.

Stan Higley ("God Is on My Pillow") lives in Fairport, New York, where he writes fiction, creative nonfiction, poetry, and humor. Stan has published more than one hundred short stories.

Carol D. Hoener ("Most High Connections") is married to her "Mr. Wonderful," James G. Hoener. She is the author of the book *Hidden Treasures* and is currently serving our Most High God through her ministry, Most High Connections.

Larkin Huey ("The Ultimate Sacrifice") has written the novel *Where the Buffalo Roam* and the short-story collection *Tales of the Tavern*, both of which are available on disk. Some of his short fiction has appeared in various anthologies and magazines. He has a master's degree in psychology and is an adjunct professor at Southern Union SCC. He lives in Roanoke, Alabama. Contact him at larkinhuey@yahoo.com.

Linda Darby Hughes ("I Have Seen Him"): Thirty-eight years of loving marriage, 106 kids (including foster, adopted, and biological), and countless blessings assure that Linda has plenty to write about for years to come. Contact her at dathasgirl@comcast.net.

Debra Johanyak ("Healed from the Inside Out") is the author of *Shakespeare's World* and other publications. She teaches college writing and assists with women's ministries at Mogadore Baptist Church.

Jewell Johnson ("Now I Cry for Joy") lives in Arizona with her husband, LeRoy. They are the parents of six children and grandparents of eight. Besides writing, Jewell spends her time quilting, walking, and reading.

Brad Nesom ("Surviving the Oklahoma City Bombing") cherishes every day with the Lord, his wife, and children. He still works as a city planner and serves in many ministries. **Eva Juliuson**, in addition to writing, encourages others in a deeper prayer life. To receive regular short e-mail prayers, contact her at evajuliuson@hotmail.com.

Dr. Muriel Larson ("A Miracle for the Doctor"), author of numerous published books, writings, and songs, is a professional Christian writer, speaker, and e-mail counselor for several online publications. She has also taught at writers conferences nationwide. Visit her Web site, *http://advicedrmuriel.blogspot.com*, or e-mail her for advice Doctormuriel@aol.com.

Karin A. Lovold ("He Was There All Along") resides in Minnesota with her husband, Michael, and their three young daughters. She loves to read and write fiction and nonfiction.

Carol F. Mog ("The Christmas Cactus") holds an M.A. in Christian counseling and a B.S. in education. She is a counselor, author, and speaker and the founder of Safe Room Ministries.

Becky Lyles ("The Miracel Man") is the author of *It's a God Thing! Inspiring Stories of Life-Changing Friendships* and *On a Wing and a Prayer: Stories from Freedom Fellowship, a Prison Ministry.*

Michelle Mach ("Prayer for an Easy-Bake Oven") lives in Colorado. Her work has been published in several anthologies, including *Simple Pleasures of Friendship* and *KnitLit the Third.*

Dean Mailes ("The Red Polka-Dotted Cap") is a writer, speaker, and educator who lives in Neosho, Missouri. He loves his wife, Carol, as well as baseball and jazz music.

Maryjo Faith Morgan ("Joy in a Jelly Jar" and "A Closed Door and an Open Window") is immensely grateful to be writing full-time back in Colorado after brief sojourns in Germany and southern California. Contact her at MaryjoFaithMorgan@hotmail.com.

Rod Nichols ("The Empty Place") is a pastor, teacher, and the author of *God's Prosperity Plan* and *Walking with God.* For more of Rod's writing, visit *www.RodNichols.com.*

Susie M. Paige ("Prescription for Rest: Remember the Sabbath") has edited the collection *Don't You Need Some*

Rest: 52 Sabbath Reflections for Stressful Living. To share your story, visit her online at susiepaige.com.

Laurie Perkins ("Stretching My Prayer Muscle") lives with her husband, Philip, in Massachusetts. A former children's librarian, Laurie dances with an expressive worship team and is writing her first novel.

Raelene Phillips ("God Cares about Christmas") is an inspirational speaker and author of *The Freedom Trilogy, Puppy in the Pulpit, Birds in the Belfry,* and *Where Is Your Pineapple?*

Evelyn Rhodes Smith ("He Hears and Answers") resides in Charleston, West Virginia, with her husband, Ted. In addition to being a freelance writer, Evelyn is a retired laboratory technician, the leader of women's Bible study groups, and a women's conference speaker.

Deborah M. Ritz ("God's Perfect Timing") is a writer and educator whose work has appeared in several *Chicken Soup for the Soul* books as well as *American Girl* magazine. She can be reached at dr@moonlitwaters.com.

Mary Catherine Rogers ("Without a Doubt") was born in New Jersey but grew up in Georgia. She is an award-winning writer and contributes feature columns to local newspapers.

C. Carletta Sanders ("Fear Not") is a stay-at-home mother of two. She resides with her husband in McKinney, Texas.

Connie R. Smith ("God Reads E-Mail") was born in beautiful Medford, Wisconsin, in 1950. She has five grown children and twelve wonderful grandchildren, two of whom she has custody. Connie has always loved to write and hopes to have more stories published.

Donna Surgenor Reames ("Finding God in a Ladybug's Wings") is a single mother with three daughters, Zoe, Chloe, and Caroline. She lives in Charleston, South Carolina, and her writing has been published in numerous magazines.

Sharon Dolores Thaniel ("Gambler or Believer?") enjoys serving God and spreading His Word. Sharon is currently completing her first children's Christian book, to be published this year.

Mrs. C. A. Tucker ("Though He Stumble . . . ") has been actively involved in writing, teaching, and preaching for various churches in both Zimbabwe and England.

Diane Meredith Vogel ("A Call for Help") lives in rural Michigan. She and her husband rehab houses and spread the gospel. This is her third *Cup of Comfort* appearance.

Christine P. Wang ("A Well-Lit Road") is a freelance writer and assistant editor for two trade magazines. She taught English as a Second Language in Hawaii, Tennessee, and New Jersey for eight years.

Ruth I. Danner Wilson ("A Piece of Blue Ribbon") and her husband have been foster parents to 140 children and now direct their attentions to the World Bible College mission in India.

Karen Witemeyer ("Dousing the Devil's Darts") is a graduate of Abilene Christian University as well as a wife and mother who loves to glorify God through music and the written word.

Joy Wooderson ("What I Learned from a Pony") emigrated from South Africa in 1971. She loves international travel and fast cars and is currently seeking publication of her award-winning memoir, *Finding Joy*.

Pauline Zeilenga ("The Master's Voice") is a freelance writer living in the Chicago area with her husband and their two children, Sarah and Chad. She is currently working on her first novel and a collection of short stories.

Tell Your Story in the Next *Cup of Comfort*!

We hope you have enjoyed *A Cup of Comfort for Christians* and that you will share it with all the special people in your life.

You won't want to miss our newest heartwarming volumes, *A Cup of Comfort for Nurses* and *A Cup of Comfort for Women in Love*. Look for these new books in your favorite bookstores soon!

We're brewing up lots of other *Cup of Comfort* books, each filled to the brim with true stories that will touch your heart and soothe your soul. The inspiring tales included in these collections are written by everyday men and women, and we would love to include one of your stories in an upcoming edition of *A Cup of Comfort*.

Do you have a powerful story about an experience that dramatically changed or enhanced your life? A compelling story that can stir our emotions, make us think, and bring us hope? An inspiring story that reveals lessons of humility within a vividly told tale? Tell us your story!

Each *Cup of Comfort* contributor will receive a monetary fee, author credit, and a complimentary copy of the book. Just e-mail your submission of 1,000 to 2,000 words (one story per e-mail; no attachments, please) to:

cupofcomfort@adamsmedia.com

Or, if e-mail is unavailable to you, send it to:

A Cup of Comfort
Adams Media
57 Littlefield Street
Avon, MA 02322

You can submit as many stories as you'd like, for whichever volumes you'd like. Make sure to include your name, address, and other contact information and indicate for which volume you'd like your story to be considered. We also welcome your suggestions or stories for new *Cup of Comfort* themes.

For more information, please visit our Web site: *www.cupofcomfort.com.*

We look forward to sharing many more soothing *Cups of Comfort* with you!